Page		FOCUS		TEXT		WHEN			WHY									HOW			
		Comprehension	Vocabulary	Narrative	Informational	Before Reading	During Reading	After Reading	Predicting	Connecting	Questioning	Using Text Structure	Visualizing	Inferring	Summarizing	Synthesizing	Determining Importance	Individual	Partner	Small Group	Whole Group
145	Prediction Chart	•		•	•	•	•		•		•							•	•	•	•
153	Putting Clues Together	•		•	•	•	•		•			•	•				•	•			
157	Question-Answer Relationships (QAR)	•		•	•	•		•	•	•	•	•		•		•		•			•
165	Questioning the Author (QTA)	•		•	•		•				•			•	•			•	•	•	•
171	Reciprocal Teaching	•		•	•	•	•	•	•		•			•	•			•	•	•	•
177	RIVET		•	•	•	•			•												•
181	Semantic Feature Analysis (SFA)		•	•	•	•			•	•	•					•					
187	Semantic Mapping	•	•	•	•	•	•	•		•					•	•	•			•	
195	Sketch to Stretch	•		•	•			•		•			•	•						•	•
201	Stop, Predict, Support (SPS)	•		•	•	•	•	•	•	•					•			•	•	•	•
207	Story Board	•		•	•			•			•	•			•			•	•	•	•
213	Story Maps	•		•				•			•	•				•		•			
219	Story Pyramid	•		•				•		•					•	•		•	•	•	•
225	Strategy Gloves	•		•	•		•	•			•	•				•		•	•	•	•
231	Text Feature Survey	•			•	•						•						•	•	•	•
237	Text Talk	•	•	•				•	•	•	•			•	•					•	•
245	Three-Phrase Map	•			•			•							•	•	•	•	•	•	•
249	Tiered Bingo	•	•	•	•	•	•	•	•	•	•				•	•	•	•			
255	Venn Diagram	•		•	•	•	•	•	•					•				•	•	•	
265	Vocabulary Anchors		•	•	•	•			•	•										•	•
271	Vocabulary Four Square		•	•	•			•				•						•	•	•	•
277	Vocabulary Self-Collection (VSS)		•	•	•			•		•							•	•	•	•	•
281	Word Sorts	•	•	•	•	•	•		•		•	•						•	•	•	

Second Edition

Comprehension
and
Vocabulary Strategies

for the Elementary Grades

Jerry L. Johns

Susan Davis Lenski

Roberta L. Berglund

KENDALL/HUNT PUBLISHING COMPANY
4050 Westmark Drive Dubuque, Iowa 52002

Book Team
Chairman and Chief Executive Officer   Mark C. Falb
Vice President, Director of National Book Program   Alfred C. Grisanti
Senior Vice President College Division   Thomas W. Gantz
Editorial Developmental Manager   Georgia Botsford
Prepress Project Coordinator   Carrie Maro
Cover Design   Jenifer Chapman

Ordering Information
Address: Kendall/Hunt Publishing Company
            4050 Westmark Drive
            Dubuque, IA 52004

Telephone: 800-247-3458, ext. 4 or 5

Web site: www.kendallhunt.com

Fax: 800-772-9165

Author Addresses for Correspondence and Workshops

Jerry L. Johns
Consultant in Reading
E-mail: *jjohns@niu.edu*
FAX: 815-899-3022

Susan Davis Lenski
Professor
Portland State University
Graduate School of Education
615 SW Harrison
Portland, OR 97207-0751
E-mail: *sjlenski@pdx.edu*
503-725-5403

Roberta L. Berglund
Consultant in Reading/Language Arts
E-mail: *bberglund@rocketmail.com*

Previously entitled *Comprehension and Vocabulary Strategies for the Primary Grades*

Copyright © 2003, 2006 by Kendall/Hunt Publishing Company

ISBN 13: 978-0-7575-2798-2
ISBN 10: 0-7575-2798-1

Printed in the United States of America

10 9 8 7 6 5 4 3 2 1

Preface and Overview

Who Will Use This Book?

We have written this practical and useful book for inservice and preservice teachers. The book is ideal for professional development in schools, districts, and other types of programs where the focus is on comprehension and vocabulary instruction in the elementary grades. It will also be a helpful supplement in undergraduate and graduate reading and language arts classes, as well as in clinical courses where there is a desire to provide useful strategies that have wide applicability with narrative and informational text.

What Are Some of the Outstanding Qualities of This Book?

1. The book contains comprehension and vocabulary strategies that have utility in reading as well as other areas of the curriculum.
2. The strategies are presented with a unique and helpful chart that quickly shows when, why, and how to use them. The chart also indicates whether the strategy can be used with narrative text, informational text, or both.
3. The strategies are presented in an easy-to-follow, step-by-step manner.
4. Most of the strategies contain one or more examples.
5. A reproducible master accompanies most strategies.
6. A CD-ROM contains all the reproducibles in the book as well as bonus reproducibles for some of the strategies.

What Grade Levels Do the Strategies Address?

The strategies in this book were specifically written for use in the elementary grades. After reading about a strategy, it should be quite easy for you to determine how best to use it with your students. You will probably want to adapt some of the strategies to fit your teaching style and your students' particular needs. For beginning readers, the strategies may be used with materials you read to students. You can then complete the strategy through shared reading and writing. Older students will be able, after appropriate instruction, to use the strategies independently.

What Insights Have Been Provided by Research?

There is little doubt that teaching results in student learning. A persistent problem is that of teachers mentioning a skill or assigning a task without taking the time to teach it. Instruction that is characterized by clear explanation, modeling, and guided practice can increase student learning (Duffy, 2002, 2003). The National Reading Panel (2000) compiled a large volume that offers several strategies for effective comprehension instruction. According to Cunningham (2001), the comprehension section of the report is potentially valuable. Other major reviews (Pearson & Fielding, 1991; Tierney & Cunningham, 1984) and related writings (Ogle & Blachowicz, 2002; Pressley, 2000, 2002, 2005; Rand Study Group, 2002) support the following areas for an instructional focus.

1. Teach students to be aware of their own comprehension. This strategy is often referred to as comprehension monitoring.
2. Have students work together. This strategy is called cooperative learning.

3. Have students make graphic summaries of what they read through the use of graphic and semantic organizers.

4. Use story and text structure.

5. Help students learn to ask and answer questions.

6. Teach students to summarize what they read.

Vocabulary knowledge plays a crucial, but complex, role in reading comprehension. The educational community has known for decades that vocabulary knowledge can strongly influence reading comprehension (Davis, 1944; Herma & Dole, 2005; Nagy & Scott, 2000). Research has shown that a relationship between vocabulary and comprehension exists (McKeown, Beck, Omanson, & Perfetti, 1983; McKeown, Beck, Omanson, & Pople, 1985; Tomeson & Aarnouste, 1998), and vocabulary instruction can play at least a partial role in that relationship (NRP, 2000). Marzano (2004) notes that "there is a growing body of evidence that vocabulary knowledge is a causal determinant of differences in reading ability in general and comprehension specifically" (pp. 100–101). Research also indicates that vocabulary instruction should provide students with a variety of rich experiences with words (Stahl & Fairbanks, 1986). Unfortunately, classroom instruction on vocabulary knowledge tends to be traditional, such as providing students with lists of words to look up in a dictionary (Blachowicz & Fisher, 2000, 2006). This simplistic reaction to the complexity of learning words, particularly as it relates to texts with vocabulary density, can hinder students from developing a rich comprehension of text. Vocabulary instruction embedded within authentic strategy instruction, therefore, has the potential for building vocabulary awareness, vocabulary knowledge, and a better comprehension of text.

The strategies selected for this book will help you in the areas of comprehension and vocabulary instruction. The key ingredients, however, are your actions as the teacher.

• Take time to teach the strategies.

• Tell students how the strategies will help them become better readers.

• Model how the strategies are used.

• Think aloud by describing what goes on in your mind as you are using the strategy.

• Provide guided practice so students can learn how the strategy will help them understand the lesson or text.

• Reinforce students' efforts.

• Develop the strategies over time and remind students to use the strategies in a variety of contexts.

• Help students reflect on the strategies and evaluate their usefulness in various contexts.

Finally, we want to stress again the critical importance of teaching the strategies. Many of the strategies can be embedded in oral reading you share with students. This means you can teach the strategies as students are in the process of becoming independent readers.

Is This Book Easy to Use?

Yes! The format and organization of this book make it very user friendly. We have also included a Quick Reference Guide inside the front cover so you can quickly locate the various strategies and consider their use. Note that the strategies are listed in alphabetical order. In addition, there are further breakdowns of the strategies on the back cover so you can quickly locate those in comprehension, vocabulary, and both areas.

Where Should I Begin?

Glance at the Quick Reference Guide inside the front cover and on the first page. Scan the strategies and find a particular strategy that interests you. Turn to the page for that strategy. Suppose you select Character Four Square on page 27. Under the title, you will see a chart that covers five areas.

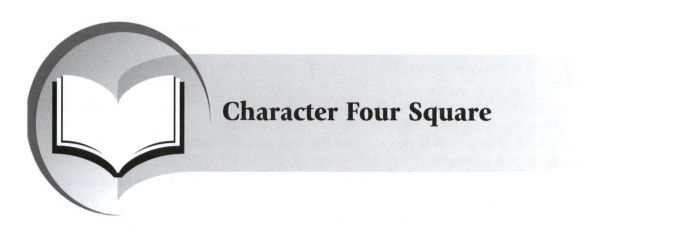

Character Four Square

FOCUS		TEXT		WHEN			WHY									HOW			
Comprehension	Vocabulary	Narrative	Informational	Before Reading	During Reading	After Reading	Predicting	Connecting	Questioning	Using Text Structure	Visualizing	Inferring	Summarizing	Synthesizing	Determining Importance	Individual	Partner	Small Group	Whole Group
•	•	•				•		•			•					•	•	•	•

1. **FOCUS** indicates which areas (i.e., comprehension and vocabulary) are covered by the strategy. The dots indicate that Character Four Square focuses on both comprehension and vocabulary.

2. **TEXT** refers to the type of text materials with which the strategies can be used. Narrative text refers to stories; informational text generally refers to nonfiction materials. The dot indicates Character Four Square would be best used with narrative materials.

3. **WHEN** tells you if you should use the strategy before, during, and/or after reading. The dot signifies that Character Four Square is best used after reading.

4. **WHY** is based on the work of Duke and Pearson (2002), Keene and Zimmermann (1997), Pearson, Roehler, Dole, and Duffy (1992) and others who have reviewed the research in comprehension. These areas help students become thoughtful, independent readers who are engaged in their reading and learning. Following are brief descriptions of the nine areas we use in this book.

   • *Predicting*—Students can make predictions about the content of a text from the title, illustrations, and headings. Students can also use their prior knowledge to anticipate word meanings or how words might be related.

   • *Connecting*—Students increase their comprehension when they think about how their lives are connected to the text and to the world.

- *Questioning*—Asking questions engages students in an internal dialogue to clarify understanding. Questions can also be asked by teachers and other students.
- *Using Text Structure*—Narrative and informational texts are organized differently. Students can use their knowledge of text structure to help understand and remember what the author wrote.
- *Visualizing*—Students can create visual images based on words from the text. These images may be shared through discussions, sketches, or drawings.
- *Inferring*—Students use what is known, as well as clues from the text, to contemplate and hypothesize about what was read.
- *Summarizing*—Students can summarize while they read and after they read to better understand the author's message.
- *Synthesizing*—Students use new information and their prior knowledge to create thoughts or perspectives.
- *Determining Importance*—Students learn to identify the important ideas in printed materials and separate them from ideas that are less important.

Character Four Square gives students an opportunity to use the processes of connecting and visualizing.

5. **HOW** refers to whether the strategy is best used with individuals, partners, small groups, and/or whole groups. Character Four Square can be used with individuals, partners, small groups, and whole groups.

Below the chart are the words *Description, Teaching Goals,* and *Procedure.* There is a brief description of Character Four Square, three teaching goals, and a step-by-step procedure for using Character Four Square. We like to think of the numbered steps as a systematic lesson plan to help you present the strategy to your students. You should, of course, feel free to adapt the steps and examples to fit your class.

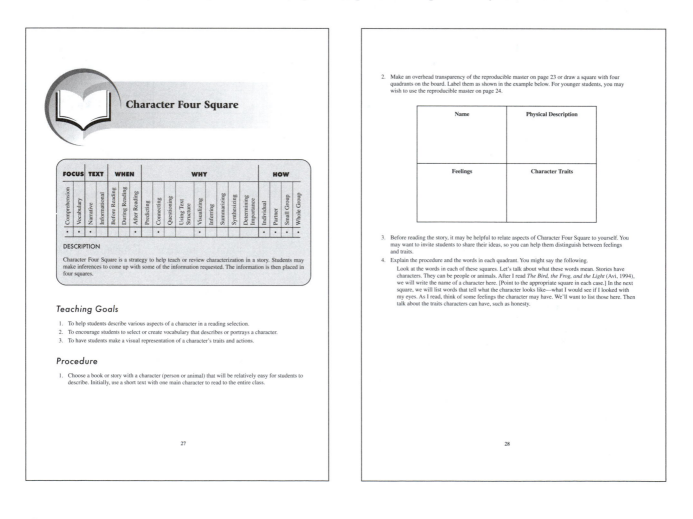

Character Four Square

| FOCUS | TEXT | WHEN | WHY | HOW |

DESCRIPTION

Character Four Square is a strategy to help teach or review characterization in a story. Students may make inferences to come up with some of the information requested. The information is then placed in four squares.

Teaching Goals

1. To help students describe various aspects of a character in a reading selection.
2. To encourage students to select or create vocabulary that describes or portrays a character.
3. To have students make a visual representation of a character's traits and actions.

Procedure

1. Choose a book or story with a character (person or animal) that will be relatively easy for students to describe. Initially, use a short text with one main character to read to the entire class.

27

2. Make an overhead transparency of the reproducible master on page 23 or draw a square with four quadrants on the board. Label them as shown in the example below. For younger students, you may wish to use the reproducible master on page 24.

Name	Physical Description
Feelings	Character Traits

3. Before reading the story, it may be helpful to relate aspects of Character Four Square to yourself. You may want to invite students to share their ideas, so you can help them distinguish between feelings and traits.
4. Explain the procedure and the words in each quadrant. You might say the following.

Look at the words in each of these squares. Let's talk about what these words mean. Stories have characters. They can be people or animals. After I read *The Bird, the Frog, and the Light* (Avi, 1994), we will write the name of a character here. [Point to the appropriate square in each case.] In the next square, we will list words that tell what the character looks like—what I would see if I looked with my eyes. As I read, think of some feelings the character may have. We'll want to list those here. Then talk about the traits characters can have, such as honesty.

28

We often provide one or more *examples* (see example below) of how the strategy might be used in your curriculum. You may quickly be able to think of logical extensions to your lessons in a variety of areas.

Character Four Square
The Bird, the Frog, and the Light by Avi

Name	Physical Description
Frog	yellow toes big green bulging wore a crown
Feelings important sad	**Character Traits** bossy proud mean impatient

To make the strategy especially useful, one or more *reproducible masters* are included with most strategies. You have the publisher's permission to reproduce and use the master with your students within the guidelines noted on the copyright page of this book. The reproducibles, along with bonus reproducibles for selected strategies, are included on a CD-ROM enclosed with each book.

References

Blachowicz, C. L. Z., & Fisher, P. (2000). Vocabulary instruction. In M. L. Kamil, P. B. Mosenthal, P. D. Pearson, & R. Barr (Eds.), *Handbook of reading research* (Vol. III) (pp. 503–523). Mahwah. NJ: Erlbaum.

Blachowicz, C., & Fisher, P. (2006). *Teaching vocabulary in all classrooms* (3rd ed.). Upper Saddle River, NJ: Merrill Prentice Hall.

Cunningham, J. W. (2001). The National Reading Panel Report (Essay Book Review). *Reading Research Quarterly, 36,* 326–335.

Davis, F. B. (1944). Fundamental factors in reading comprehension. *Psychometrika, 9,* 185–197.

Duffy, G. G. (2003). *Explaining reading: A resource for teaching concepts, skills, and strategies.* New York: Guilford.

Duffy, G. G. (2002). The case for direct explanation of strategies. In C. C. Block & M. Pressley (Eds.), *Comprehension instruction: Research-based best practices* (pp. 28–41). New York: Guilford.

Duke, N. K., & Pearson, P. D. (2002). Effective practices for developing reading comprehension. In A. E. Farstrup & S. J. Samuels (Eds.), *What research has to say about reading instruction* (3rd ed.) (pp. 205–242). Newark, DE: International Reading Association.

Herma, P. A., & Dole, J. (2005). Theory and practice in vocabulary learning and instruction. In Z. Fang (Ed.), *Literacy teaching and learning: Current issues and trends* (pp. 112–120). Upper Saddle River, NJ: Pearson.

Keene, E. O., & Zimmermann, S. (1997). *Mosaic of thought.* Portsmouth, NH: Heinemann.

Marzano, R. J. (2004). The developing vision of vocabulary instruction. In J. F. Baumann & Edward J. Kame'enui (Eds.), *Vocabulary instruction: Research to practice* (pp. 100–117). New York: Guilford.

McKeown, M. G., Beck, I. L., Omanson, R. C., & Perfetti, C. A. (1983). The effects of long-term vocabulary instruction on reading comprehension: A replication. *Journal of Reading Behavior, 15,* 3–18.

McKeown, M. G., Beck, I. L., Omanson, R. C., & Pople, M. T. (1985). Some effects of the nature and frequency of vocabulary instruction on the knowledge and use of words. *Reading Research Quarterly, 20,* 522–535.

Nagy, W. E., & Scott, J. A. (2000). Vocabulary processes. In M. L. Kamil, P. B. Mosenthal, P. D. Pearson, & R. Barr (Eds.), *Handbook of reading research* (Vol. III) (pp. 269–284). Mahwah, NJ: Erlbaum.

National Reading Panel. (2000). *Teaching children to read: An evidence-based assessment of the scientific research literature on reading and its implications for reading instruction.* Washington, DC: National Institute for Child Health & Human Development.

Ogle, D., & Blachowicz, C. L. Z. (2002). Beyond literature circles: Helping students comprehend informational text. In C. C. Block & M. Pressley (Eds.), *Comprehension instruction: Research-based best practices* (pp. 259–274). New York: Guilford.

Pearson, P. D., & Fielding, L. (1991). Comprehension instruction. In R. Barr, M. L. Kamil, P. B. Mosenthal, & P. D. Pearson (Eds.), *Handbook of reading research* (Vol. II) (pp. 815–816). White Plains, NY: Longman.

Pearson, P. D., Roehler, L. R., Dole, J. A., & Duffy, G. G. (1992). Developing expertise in reading comprehension. In S. J. Samuels & A. E. Farstrup (Eds.) *What research has to say about reading instruction* (2nd ed.) (pp. 153–169). Newark, DE: International Reading Association.

Pressley, M. (2000). What should comprehension instruction be the instruction of? In M. L. Kamil, P. B. Mosenthal, P. D. Pearson, & R. Barr (Eds.), *Handbook of reading research* (Vol. III) (pp. 545–561). Mahwah, NJ: Erlbaum.

Pressley, M. (2002). Comprehension strategies instruction: A turn-of-the-century status report. In C. C. Block & M. Pressley (Eds.), *Comprehension instruction: Research-based best practices* (pp. 11–27). New York: Guilford.

Pressley, M. (2005). *Reading instruction that works: The case for balanced teaching* (3rd ed.). New York: Guilford.

Rand Study Group. (2002). *Reading for understanding: Toward an R&D program in reading comprehension.* Santa Monica, CA: Author.

Stahl, S., & Fairbanks, M. (1986). The effects of vocabulary instruction: A model-based meta-analysis. *Review of Educational Research, 56,* 72–110.

Tierney, R. J., & Cunningham, J. W. (1984). Research on teaching reading comprehension. In P. D. Pearson, R. Barr, M. L. Kamil, & P. Mosenthal (Eds.), *Handbook of reading research* (Vol. I) (pp. 609–655). White Plains, NY: Longman.

Tomesen, M., & Aarnouste, C. (1998). Effects of an instructional programme for deriving word meanings. *Educational Studies, 24,* 107–128.

Acknowledgments

We are grateful to the many professionals whose research and writing provided a basis for this book. There were also three teachers whose insights were extremely helpful.

- Theresa L. Hjelm, a teacher at George Middle School in Portland, Oregon
- Rita Shafer, a teacher at Pleasant Lane Elementary School in Lombard, Illinois
- Kim Siemers, a reading teacher at Leland Elementary School in Leland, Illinois

Jerry, Sue, and Bobbi

About the Authors

Jerry L. Johns has been recognized as a distinguished professor, writer, and outstanding teacher educator. His career was spent at Northern Illinois University along with visiting professorships at the University of Victoria in British Columbia and Western Washington University. He has taught students from kindergarten through college. Dr. Johns now serves as a consultant and speaker to schools and professional organizations.

Dr. Johns is a past president of the International Reading Association, Illinois Reading Council, College Reading Association, and Northern Illinois Reading Council. He has received recognition for outstanding service to each of these professional organizations and is a member of the Illinois Reading Council Hall of Fame. Dr. Johns has served on numerous committees of the International Reading Association (IRA) and was a member of the Board of Directors. He has also received the Outstanding Teacher Educator in Reading Award from the International Reading Association.

Dr. Johns has been invited to consult, conduct workshops, and make presentations for teachers and professional groups throughout the United States and in seven countries. He has also prepared nearly 300 publications and more than twenty books that have been useful to a diverse group of educators. His *Basic Reading Inventory,* now in its ninth edition, is widely used in undergraduate and graduate classes, as well as by practicing teachers. Dr. Johns recently coauthored the fourth edition of *Improving Reading: Strategies and Resources,* the second edition of *Improving Writing, Visualization: Using Mental Images to Strengthen Comprehension,* and the third edition of *Fluency: Strategies & Assessments.*

Susan Davis Lenski is a Professor at Portland State University (PSU) in Oregon. Before joining the faculty at PSU, Dr. Lenski taught in public schools for 20 years and at Illinois State University for 11 years. Her teaching experiences include working with children from kindergarten through high school. Dr. Lenski currently teaches graduate reading and language arts courses.

Dr. Lenski has been recognized by several organizations for her commitment to education. Among her numerous awards, Dr. Lenski was presented with the Nila Banton Smith Award from the International Reading Association (IRA); she was instrumental in her school receiving an Exemplary Reading Program Award from the IRA; and she was inducted into the Illinois Reading Hall of Fame. She is currently on the Board of Directors for IRA.

Dr. Lenski's research interests focus on strategic reading and writing and adolescent literacy. She also conducts research on preparing teacher candidates. Dr. Lenski has conducted numerous inservice presentations in the United States, Canada, Guatemala, the Philippines, and Panama and has presented at many state and national conferences. Dr. Lenski has published over 60 articles and twelve books.

Roberta L. (Bobbi) Berglund has had a long and distinguished career in education. Her public school experience spans more than 20 years and includes serving as a classroom teacher, reading specialist, Title I Director, and district curriculum administrator. Dr. Berglund has been a member of the reading faculty at the University of Wisconsin-Whitewater and has also taught graduate reading courses at Northern Illinois University, Rockford College, National-Louis University, and Aurora University. Currently Dr. Berglund is a consultant in the area of reading and language arts, working with school districts and regional offices of education in developing curriculum and assessment, conducting staff development, and guiding the selection of instructional materials for reading, spelling, writing, and related areas.

Dr. Berglund has received honors for outstanding service to several organizations and has been selected as a member of the Illinois Reading Council Hall of Fame. She also was honored with the Those Who Excel Award from the Illinois State Board of Education. Dr. Berglund has served on several committees of the International Reading Association, including the program committee for the World Congress in Scotland and as chair of the Publications Committee.

Dr. Berglund has conducted numerous workshops for teachers and has been invited to make presentations at state, national, and international conferences. She is the author of over fifty publications and is the coauthor of seven professional books, including the third edition of *Fluency: Strategies and Assessments* and the second edition of *Strategies for Content Area Learning*.

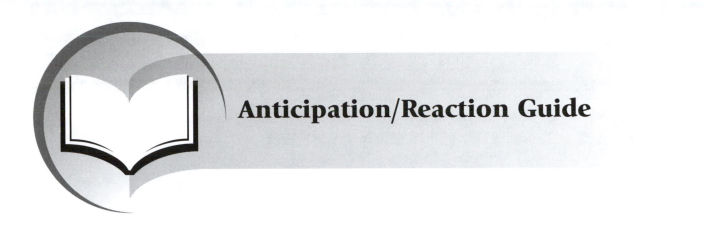

Anticipation/Reaction Guide

FOCUS		TEXT		WHEN			WHY									HOW			
Comprehension	Vocabulary	Narrative	Informational	Before Reading	During Reading	After Reading	Predicting	Connecting	Questioning	Using Text Structure	Visualizing	Inferring	Summarizing	Synthesizing	Determining Importance	Individual	Partner	Small Group	Whole Group
•		•	•	•	•	•	•	•	•			•		•		•	•	•	•

DESCRIPTION

Before students begin reading, they should activate their prior knowledge. A strategy that prompts students to think about the key concepts of a story or selection before they read is an Anticipation Guide (Herber, 1978). The key concepts can be facts that students will learn from reading, or they can be opinion statements. An Anticipation Guide can also be used after reading to confirm or alter students' ideas and is commonly called a Reaction Guide. This strategy, therefore, can help students make predictions before reading, and it can also provide a framework for checking the accuracy of the predictions during and after reading.

Teaching Goals

1. To encourage students to make connections between their background knowledge and the content of a reading selection.
2. To encourage students to make predictions.
3. To help students establish purposes for reading.
4. To provide opportunities for students to revise their predictions during and after reading.

Procedure

1. Identify a selection which you want students to read. The text should contain facts that students could learn or key concepts from which students can develop opinions.

2. List the facts or the concepts that you want students to learn. For example, if you want students to read *Pigs* by Gibbons (1991), you might list the following terms and ideas.
   - piglet
   - not dirty
   - intelligent
   - grow fast
   - not always pink

3. After you have identified terms and ideas, create sentences that could be answered with a "yes" or a "no." Do not write open-ended questions. For example, you should write, "A baby pig is called a piglet," rather than asking, "What is a baby pig called?" Some Anticipation/Reaction Guide sentences appear below.
   - A baby pig is called a piglet.
   - Pigs are smelly and dirty animals.
   - Pigs are the smartest of all farm animals.
   - Pigs grow faster than any other farm animal.
   - All pigs are pink.

4. Duplicate a copy of the blank Anticipation/Reaction Guide Sheet on page 5. Write the sentences on the lines.

5. Duplicate and distribute copies of your completed Anticipation/Reaction Guide to students. Tell students that you want to know what they think *before* reading the book *Pigs*. Emphasize that you don't expect students to know the answers, but that you want them to make their best guesses about whether the statements are correct or incorrect.

6. Read one of the statements with students. For example, read the statement "A baby pig is called a piglet." Ask them to decide whether they think the answer is "yes" or "no." Tell students to circle the answer that they think is correct to the left of the statements. Encourage students to work independently.

7. Have students read the remaining statements or read them to the students. Tell students to respond to each statement with their best guess.

8. After students have finished, tell them to read or listen to the story, paying special attention to the ideas presented in the Anticipation/Reaction Guide statements.

9. After students have read the story, have them revisit the Anticipation/Reaction Guide by reacting to the statements once more. This time have students respond to the right of the statements. After reading, discuss the idea that readers can change their minds while reading by saying something like the following.

   When you read, you have some ideas before you begin, just like we did before we read the book *Pigs*. Most of us thought that pigs are smelly and dirty before we read the story, but we found out that pigs are really very clean animals. We learned something when we read this book, so we changed our minds about the statement, "Pigs are smelly and dirty animals." After we read, we need to think about what we have learned and whether we need to change our minds about something.

10. An Anticipation/Reaction Guide using opinions rather than factual statements can be found on page 4, and a reproducible master of an Anticipation/Reaction Guide is on page 5.

11. To use an Anticipation/Reaction Guide as a study tool, help students identify all the "yes" or "true" statements after reading. Then have students use the back side of their papers to rewrite all "no" or "false" statements to make them valid.

References

Herber, H. H. (1978). *Teaching reading in the content areas* (2nd ed.). Englewood Cliffs, NJ: Prentice-Hall.

Gibbons, G. (1991). *Pigs.* New York: Scholastic.

Wyeth, S. D. (1998). *Something beautiful.* New York: Random House.

Anticipation/Reaction Guide

Something Beautiful by S. D. Wyeth

⇒ **DIRECTIONS**

Before reading or listening to the story *Something Beautiful,* decide whether you agree or disagree with each of these statements. Circle "yes" or "no." After reading, think about whether you still agree or disagree or whether you want to change your mind. Circle "yes" or "no."

Before Reading			**After Reading**	
(Yes)	No	1. Everyone should have something beautiful.	Yes	No
Yes	(No)	2. When life is hard, there's nothing you can do.	Yes	No
Yes	(No)	3. The same thing makes everyone happy.	Yes	No
(Yes)	No	4. People can find something beautiful if they try.	Yes	No

Name _____ Date _____

 # Anticipation/Reaction Guide

_____
Title and Author

⇒ DIRECTIONS

Before reading or listening, decide whether you agree or disagree with each of these statements. Circle "yes" or "no." After reading think about whether you still agree or disagree or whether you want to change your mind. Circle "yes" or "no."

Before Reading   **After Reading**

Yes   No   1. _____   Yes   No

                     _____

Yes   No   2. _____   Yes   No

                     _____

Yes   No   3. _____   Yes   No

                     _____

Yes   No   4. _____   Yes   No

                     _____

Yes   No   5. _____   Yes   No

                     _____

Yes   No   6. _____   Yes   No

                     _____

Name _____ Date _____

 # Anticipation Guide

_____
Title and Author

➤ DIRECTIONS

Before you read or listen to a selection, decide if you agree or disagree with the statements written below. Circle "Agree" or "Disagree."

Agree   Disagree   1. _____

_____

Agree   Disagree   2. _____

_____

Agree   Disagree   3. _____

_____

Agree   Disagree   4. _____

_____

Agree   Disagree   5. _____

_____

Agree   Disagree   6. _____

_____

Agree   Disagree   7. _____

_____

Agree   Disagree   8. _____

_____

Agree   Disagree   9. _____

_____

Name _____ Date _____

 **Reaction Guide**

_____
Title and Author

➣ **DIRECTIONS**

After you read or listen to a selection, decide whether you agree or disagree with the statements written below. Circle the word that fits your choice and explain why you feel as you do.

1. _____   Agree   Disagree
   _____

   Why? _____
   _____

2. _____   Agree   Disagree
   _____

   Why? _____
   _____

3. _____   Agree   Disagree
   _____

   Why? _____
   _____

4. _____   Agree   Disagree
   _____

   Why? _____
   _____

5. _____   Agree   Disagree
   _____

   Why? _____
   _____

Bookmark Strategy Prompts

FOCUS		TEXT		WHEN			WHY									HOW			
Comprehension	Vocabulary	Narrative	Informational	Before Reading	During Reading	After Reading	Predicting	Connecting	Questioning	Using Text Structure	Visualizing	Inferring	Summarizing	Synthesizing	Determining Importance	Individual	Partner	Small Group	Whole Group
•	•	•	•		•		•	•	•		•	•	•	•	•	•		•	•

DESCRIPTION

After decoding and comprehension strategies have been taught to students, there is a continuing need to give them opportunities to practice the strategies during reading. Some students may not remember the strategies or realize when a particular strategy may be useful. To help overcome these concerns, several different Bookmark Strategy Prompts are provided for your use.

Teaching Goals

1. To help students develop independence in monitoring their reading.
2. To encourage students to use a variety of strategies during reading.
3. To help students decode unknown words and comprehend reading selections.
4. To provide support for students as they use reading strategies independently.

Procedure

1. Review the different sets of Bookmark Strategy Prompts on pages 11 through 14 and duplicate the page that is most appropriate for your students; or, you can create your own prompts. The bookmarks can be duplicated on card stock and laminated so they last longer.

2. Be sure that you teach the various strategies on a particular bookmark before using the Bookmark Strategy Prompts. You can focus on a single strategy initially and then add additional strategies in subsequent lessons. General guidelines for teaching each strategy are listed below.

   - Create an awareness of the strategy. Help students understand how learning and using the strategy will make them better readers.

   - Define or explain the strategy using terminology that students will understand.

   - Model the strategy with instructional materials in your classroom. One way to model is to think aloud as you process the information.

   - Provide students practice in the use of the strategy through the use of interesting and appropriate materials.

   - Encourage students to use the strategy as they engage in a wide variety of reading situations. The Bookmark Strategy Prompts are very useful reminders of strategies that can be used.

3. Use the bookmark with the whole group, smaller groups who read at approximately the same level, or groups who may need to learn or practice a particular strategy. As you teach the strategy, you might say something like the following.

   Today in our group we are going to use our bookmark while we read. There are many ideas on the bookmark to help us know what to do when we read. We are going to focus on the idea titled "fix my mistakes." Take a crayon or marker and circle that item on your bookmark. [Take time to review what the phrase "fix my mistakes" means. See bookmark on page 12.]

4. Have students read the first page in the selected text silently. They should pay particular attention to any mistakes they made and what they do to fix them (or to try to fix them). After students have read the page, allow time for them to share their mistakes and the strategies they used to make sense of their reading. A sample interchange follows.

   Mrs. West: Let's share what we did to fix our mistakes.

   Cote: I first read *eat* [for *munch*] because the picture showed the children eating. It didn't make sense to say *eat on carrots,* so I went back and reread the sentence and came up with the word *munch.* It made sense and looked like the right word.

   David: I wasn't sure if I pronounced *Lin* correctly. I said it like Lynn in our room, but the words are spelled differently. I think I'm correct. Am I?

   Mrs. West: Yes, you are correct. It was very good that you were able to relate *Lin* to another word you knew.

5. Use a similar approach with other elements on the Bookmark Strategy Prompts. As students develop greater competence with the strategies, encourage their use during independent reading. From time to time, it is also a good idea to model the bookmark elements during instruction with small groups or the entire class.

What's the word?

What can I do when I'm stuck on a word?

1. Look at the pictures.

2. Get your mouth ready for the beginning sound.

3. Read on and come back to the word.

4. Put in a word that would make sense.

5. Look for the little parts that I know.
   CANDY
   C-AND-Y

6. Ask someone for help.

What's the word?

What can I do when I'm stuck on a word?

1. Look at the pictures.

2. Get your mouth ready for the beginning sound.

3. Read on and come back to the word.

4. Put in a word that would make sense.

5. Look for the little parts that I know.
   CANDY
   C-AND-Y

6. Ask someone for help.

What's the word?

What can I do when I'm stuck on a word?

1. Look at the pictures.

2. Get your mouth ready for the beginning sound.

3. Read on and come back to the word.

4. Put in a word that would make sense.

5. Look for the little parts that I know.
   CANDY
   C-AND-Y

6. Ask someone for help.

What can I do to understand what I read?

1. Make a prediction and check to see if I am right.

2. Try to make a picture in my head.

3. Look at pictures in the book.

4. Think about what is happening.

5. Look for words I know.

6. Look at word bits and parts.

7. Fix my mistakes.

8. Read ahead.

9. Read it again to myself.

10. Read it again aloud.

11. Remember what happened first, next, and last.

12. Tell what it is about in a sentence.

13. Think, "Does this make sense?"

What can I do to understand what I read?

1. Make a prediction and check to see if I am right.

2. Try to make a picture in my head.

3. Look at pictures in the book.

4. Think about what is happening.

5. Look for words I know.

6. Look at word bits and parts.

7. Fix my mistakes.

8. Read ahead.

9. Read it again to myself.

10. Read it again aloud.

11. Remember what happened first, next, and last.

12. Tell what it is about in a sentence.

13. Think, "Does this make sense?"

What can I do to understand what I read?

1. Make a prediction and check to see if I am right.

2. Try to make a picture in my head.

3. Look at pictures in the book.

4. Think about what is happening.

5. Look for words I know.

6. Look at word bits and parts.

7. Fix my mistakes.

8. Read ahead.

9. Read it again to myself.

10. Read it again aloud.

11. Remember what happened first, next, and last.

12. Tell what it is about in a sentence.

13. Think, "Does this make sense?"

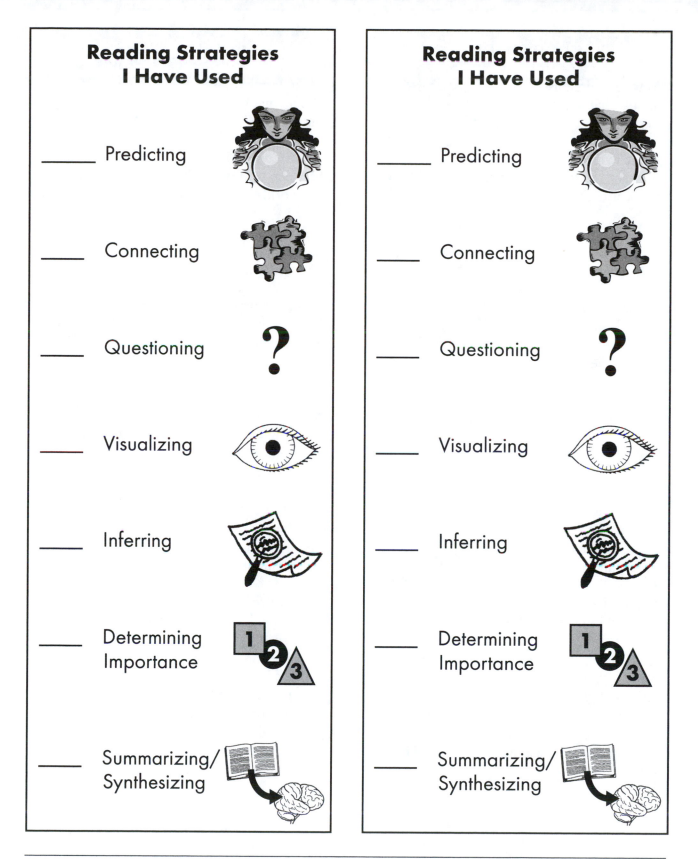

Reading Strategies
I Have Used

_____ Predicting

_____ Connecting

_____ Questioning

_____ Visualizing

_____ Inferring

_____ Determining Importance

_____ Summarizing/ Synthesizing

Reading Strategies
I Have Used

_____ Predicting

_____ Connecting

_____ Questioning

_____ Visualizing

_____ Inferring

_____ Determining Importance

_____ Summarizing/ Synthesizing

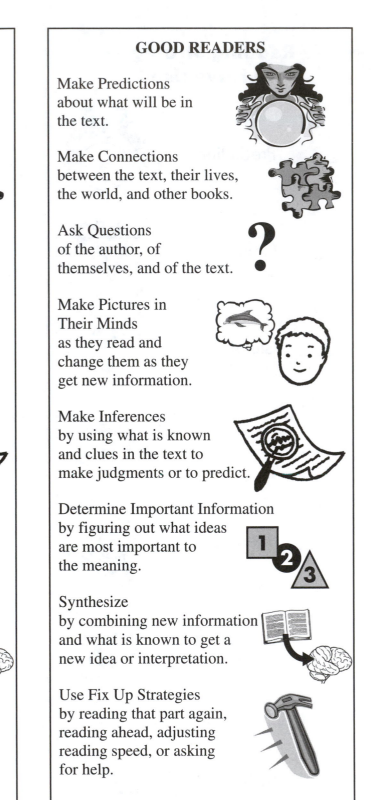

GOOD READERS

Make Predictions
about what will be in
the text.

Make Connections
between the text, their lives,
the world, and other books.

Ask Questions
of the author, of
themselves, and of the text.

**Make Pictures in
Their Minds**
as they read and
change them as they
get new information.

Make Inferences
by using what is known
and clues in the text to
make judgments or to predict.

Determine Important Information
by figuring out what ideas
are most important to
the meaning.

Synthesize
by combining new information
and what is known to get a
new idea or interpretation.

Use Fix Up Strategies
by reading that part again,
reading ahead, adjusting
reading speed, or asking
for help.

GOOD READERS

Make Predictions
about what will be in
the text.

Make Connections
between the text, their lives,
the world, and other books.

Ask Questions
of the author, of
themselves, and of the text.

**Make Pictures in
Their Minds**
as they read and
change them as they
get new information.

Make Inferences
by using what is known
and clues in the text to
make judgments or to predict.

Determine Important Information
by figuring out what ideas
are most important to
the meaning.

Synthesize
by combining new information
and what is known to get a
new idea or interpretation.

Use Fix Up Strategies
by reading that part again,
reading ahead, adjusting
reading speed, or asking
for help.

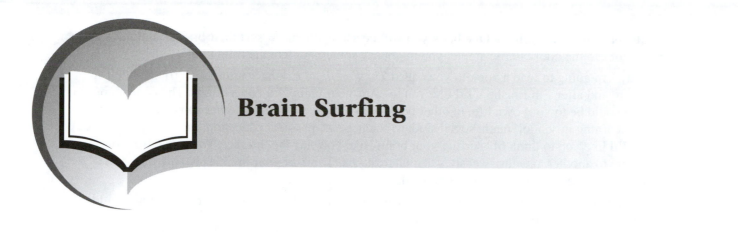

Brain Surfing

FOCUS		TEXT		WHEN			WHY									HOW			
Comprehension	Vocabulary	Narrative	Informational	Before Reading	During Reading	After Reading	Predicting	Connecting	Questioning	Using Text Structure	Visualizing	Inferring	Summarizing	Synthesizing	Determining Importance	Individual	Partner	Small Group	Whole Group
•	•	•			•	•		•	•				•	•		•	•	•	•

DESCRIPTION

Students' reading comprehension can be enriched when they discuss their interpretations of stories after reading. Strategies that help students make connections to their lives, to other texts, and to the subjects that they've been learning are especially valuable. One strategy that fosters connections after reading is Brain Surfing (Lenski, 2001). Brain Surfing encourages students to think about meanings after reading by "surfing" their brain like they would surf the Internet for material.

Teaching Goals

1. To help students make connections from their reading to other subjects taught in schools.
2. To increase students' awareness of ways school subjects relate to each other.
3. To deepen students' understanding of multiple ways of comprehending texts.

Procedure

1. Identify a book that you would like to read to your class or that you want your students to read silently. If students read the book silently, make sure the book is at a level that everyone can comprehend. Choose books that have the potential for connections to all subject areas that you teach.
2. Duplicate and distribute a reproducible master of the Brain Surfing graphic on page 18 or draw the graphic on the board.

3. Tell students that after you read the book you will be asking them to "surf their brains" and think about connections to the book. For example, you might say something like the following.

   Today I'm going to read a book to you called *The Family of Earth* (Schimmel, 2001). While I'm reading and after I'm finished, I'd like you to "surf your brain" for connections. The connections you make could be to your own life, to other books you have read, or to the other subjects that we've been learning in school: math, social studies, science, art, physical education, music, and language arts. I'd like you to think of "surfing your brain" like you surf the Internet. You move from one website to another, opening websites that interest you. Think of your brain as having different websites for each of the areas we discussed.

4. Draw students' attention to the Brain Surfing sheet. Identify each of the areas for which they could make a connection. Tell students something like the following.

   You can see on the graphic that we have circles of each of the areas where you'll be making connections. While I'm reading *The Family of Earth,* I'd like you to "surf your brains" and think of connections to each of these areas. If you make a connection, write it down in the circle so that you remember your connections for our class discussion after I finish reading.

5. Begin reading the book to students. Stop periodically and invite students to make connections.

6. After reading, provide students with a few more minutes to make connections and write them on the Brain Surfing sheet. Then discuss the connections students have made. A sample class discussion follows.

   Mrs. Kinzinger: What connections did you make to *The Family of Earth?*

   Tamika: The first picture reminded me of the space unit we had last year. I remember pictures of the earth and moon taken from space like that picture.

   Mrs. Kinzinger: What area of the Brain Surfing sheet would that be?

   Tamika: It would be the science area.

   Mrs. Kinzinger: Let's write "space unit" in the science circle.

7. As you discuss students' connections with them, prompt them to think about areas of connections that they did not make. Provide them with your own connections if they are unable to make any. A sample discussion illustrating a prompt follows.

   Mrs. Kinzinger: No one made connections from *The Family of Earth* to music. Was anyone reminded of a song while they were reading?

   (No response.)

   Mrs. Kinzinger: Sometimes when I'm reading, music plays in my head. Often the music relates to the story, but sometimes it's a little different. When I was reading *The Family of Earth,* the song "We Are the World" came into my head. I've brought that song to play for you. [Play a recording of the song.] As you read, try to think of as many different kinds of connections as you can. If you "surf your brain," you'll be amazed at the different connections that you can make.

8. Encourage students to make connections on their own during and after reading. The Brain Surfing reproducible master can prompt students' attention to the various areas where they can connect their learning from the new book to their prior knowledge.

9. A sample Brain Surfing sheet for *The Family of Earth* and reproducible masters of the Brain Surfing graphic can be found on pages 17–19.

References

Lenski, S. D. (2001). Brain surfing: A strategy for making cross-curricular connections. *Reading Horizons, 42,* 21–37.

Schimmel, S. (2001). *The family of earth.* Minnetonka, MN: NorthWord Press.

Brain Surfing

The Family of Earth by S. Schimmel

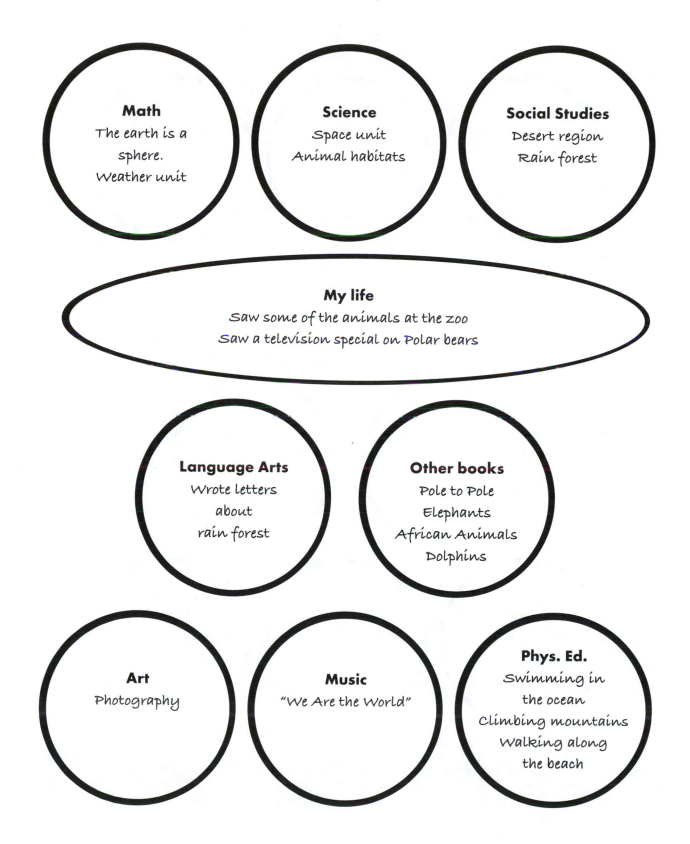

Math
The earth is a sphere.
Weather unit

Science
Space unit
Animal habitats

Social Studies
Desert region
Rain forest

My life
Saw some of the animals at the zoo
Saw a television special on Polar bears

Language Arts
Wrote letters about rain forest

Other books
Pole to Pole
Elephants
African Animals
Dolphins

Art
Photography

Music
"We Are the World"

Phys. Ed.
Swimming in the ocean
Climbing mountains
Walking along the beach

Name _____   Date _____

  Brain Surfing

_____
Title and Author

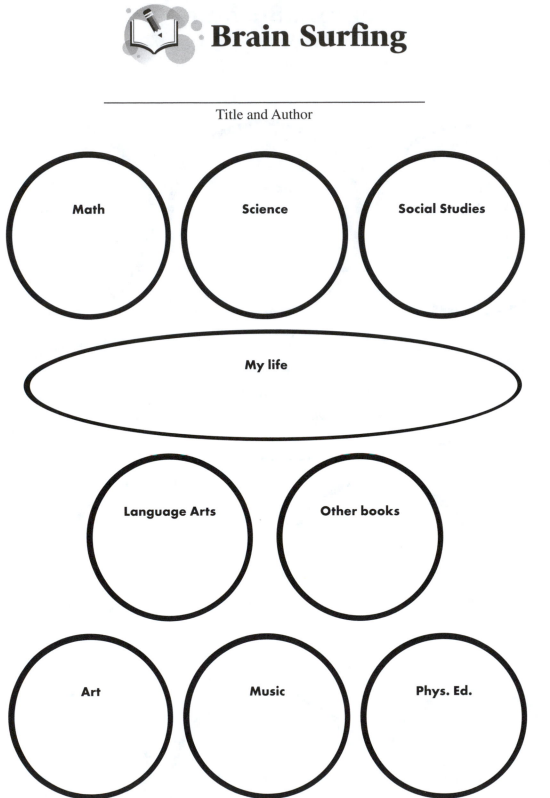

Name _____ Date _____

Brain Surfing

_____
Title and Author

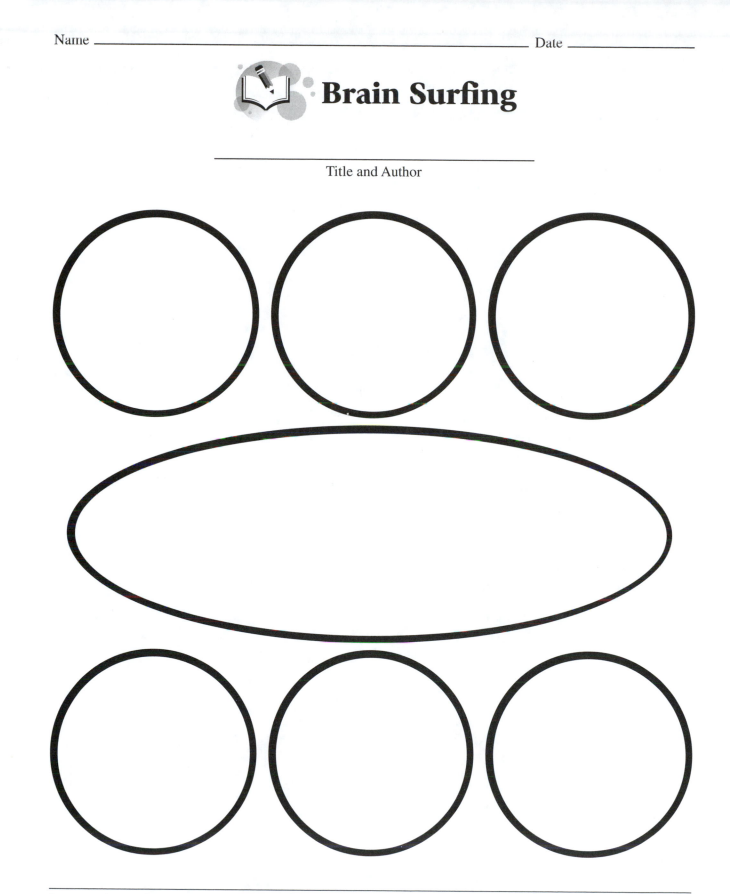

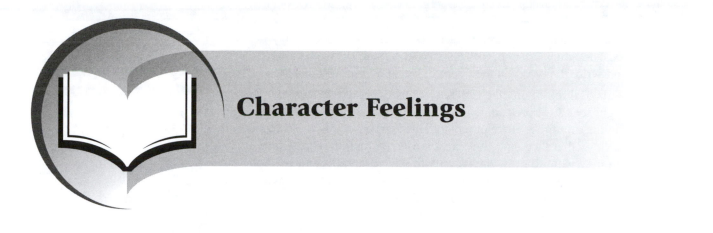

Character Feelings

FOCUS		TEXT		WHEN			WHY									HOW			
Comprehension	Vocabulary	Narrative	Informational	Before Reading	During Reading	After Reading	Predicting	Connecting	Questioning	Using Text Structure	Visualizing	Inferring	Summarizing	Synthesizing	Determining Importance	Individual	Partner	Small Group	Whole Group
•		•				•					•	•		•		•		•	•

DESCRIPTION

Character Feelings, based on Johns and Berglund (2006) and Johns and Lenski (2005), can be used with fictional characters, real people, or biographical sketches. Students' identification of the feelings should be based on an analysis of the printed material. Students should also provide evidence for their decisions.

Teaching Goals

1. To help students identify a character's feelings using stated and implied information in a reading selection.
2. To encourage students to visualize how a character might feel.

Procedure

1. Identify a particular narrative selection that can be read with or to students. When doing this activity for the first time, you may want to choose a selection that has only one main character. Kindergarten and first-grade teachers may want to have a Big Book to read to students. Second- and third-grade teachers may want to provide either a personal copy of the selection for students or use a large copy with the entire class. Older students can read the selection independently.

2. Draw or show a picture of a smiley face. Ask students what a smiley face represents. They may say happiness or joy. Accept any reasonable answer and write the word on the board or on an overhead transparency.

3. Ask students to think of any faces they can make that would show how a person might feel. Call on a student to show his or her face to the class without saying anything. Have other students "guess" what face is being presented, draw that face, and write an appropriate feeling word on the board. You may want to draw the faces with other emotions and write the feeling word next to it. Continue with this activity until students have made all the faces they can think of at that time. Some possibilities are listed in the sidebar to the right.

4. Have students read the selection or read the selection to them. After reading the selection, have students draw (or circle) the face(s) they think represents the feelings of the character. This can be done on the reproducible master or on the board. Older students can write a short reminder of clues in the story. A face could be drawn in the margin next to the text that supports the feeling.

5. If your reading selection has several characters, you might also have students discuss the feelings of those characters.

References

Johns, J. L., & Berglund, R. L. (2006). *Strategies for content area learning* (2nd ed.). Dubuque, IA: Kendall/Hunt.

Johns, J. L., & Lenski, S. D. (2005). *Improving reading: Strategies and resources* (4th ed.). Dubuque, IA: Kendall/Hunt.

Name _____ Date _____

 # Character Feelings

⟹ **DIRECTIONS**

Choose a character in the story. Circle the word that tells how the character in the story felt and draw the face to show that feeling.

Character's Name _____

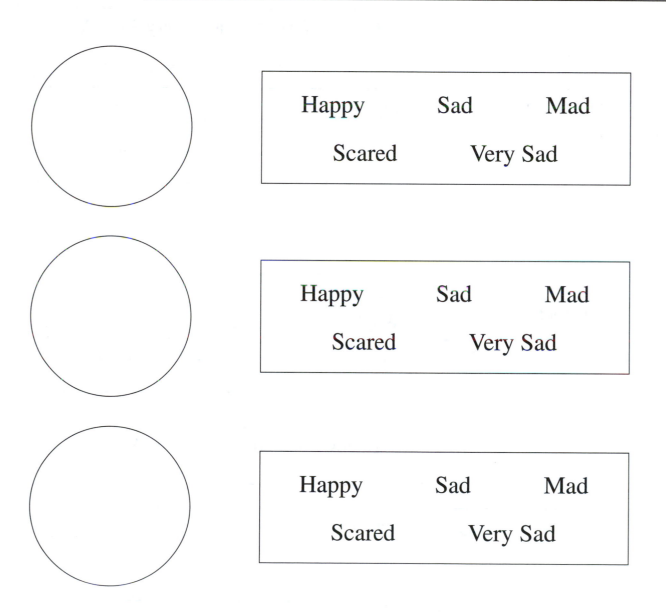

Happy	Sad	Mad
Scared	Very Sad	

Happy	Sad	Mad
Scared	Very Sad	

Happy	Sad	Mad
Scared	Very Sad	

Name _____ Date _____

Character Feelings

Choose some characters in the story. Write the name of the character on the line. Circle the word in the box that tells how the character in the story felt or add words to describe how the character felt. Then explain why the character had that feeling.

_____

Character

Happy	Scared	Sad	Very Sad	Mad
_____			_____	

Why? _____

_____

_____

_____

Character

Happy	Scared	Sad	Very Sad	Mad
_____			_____	

Why? _____

_____

_____

_____

Character

Happy	Scared	Sad	Very Sad	Mad
_____			_____	

Why? _____

_____

_____

Name _____ Date _____

Changes in Character Feelings

➥ DIRECTIONS

Choose two or more characters in the story. Write the name of the first character on the line. Then think of feelings the character had at the beginning, middle, and end of the story. Write the feelings on the line. Explain why the character's feelings changed or did not change. Then do the same thing for any other characters you selected.

_____

Character

| _____ | _____ | _____ |
| Beginning of Story | Middle of Story | End of Story |

The character's feelings _____

_____

Character

| _____ | _____ | _____ |
| Beginning of Story | Middle of Story | End of Story |

The character's feelings _____

_____

Character

| _____ | _____ | _____ |
| Beginning of Story | Middle of Story | End of Story |

The character's feelings _____

Jerry L. Johns, Susan Davis Lenski, and Roberta L. Berglund. *Comprehension and Vocabulary Strategies for the Elementary Grades* (2nd ed.). Copyright © 2006 by Kendall/Hunt Publishing Company (1-800-247-3458, ext. 4).

Name _____   Date _____

Changes in Character Feelings

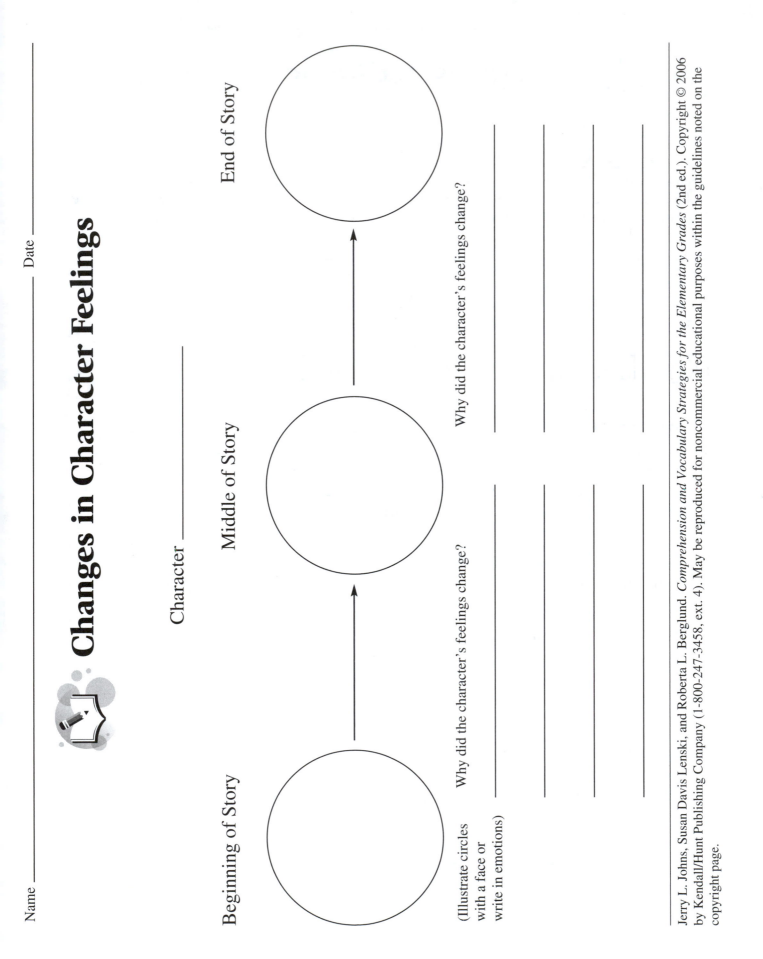

Character _____

Beginning of Story

Middle of Story

End of Story

(Illustrate circles with a face or write in emotions)

Why did the character's feelings change?

_____

_____

Why did the character's feelings change?

_____

_____

_____

Jerry L. Johns, Susan Davis Lenski, and Roberta L. Berglund. *Comprehension and Vocabulary Strategies for the Elementary Grades* (2nd ed.). Copyright © 2006 by Kendall/Hunt Publishing Company (1-800-247-3458, ext. 4). May be reproduced for noncommercial educational purposes within the guidelines noted on the copyright page.

26

Character Four Square

FOCUS		TEXT		WHEN			WHY									HOW			
Comprehension	Vocabulary	Narrative	Informational	Before Reading	During Reading	After Reading	Predicting	Connecting	Questioning	Using Text Structure	Visualizing	Inferring	Summarizing	Synthesizing	Determining Importance	Individual	Partner	Small Group	Whole Group
•	•	•				•		•			•	•				•	•	•	•

DESCRIPTION

Character Four Square is a strategy to help teach or review characterization in a story. Students can make inferences to come up with some of the information requested. The information is then placed in four squares.

Teaching Goals

1. To help students describe various aspects of a character in a reading selection.
2. To encourage students to select or create vocabulary that describes or portrays a character.
3. To have students make a visual representation of a character's traits and actions.

Procedure

1. Choose a book or story with a character (person or animal) that will be relatively easy for students to describe. Initially, use a short text with one main character to read to the entire class.

2. Make an overhead transparency of the reproducible master on page 30 or draw a square with four quadrants on the board. Label them as shown in the example below. For younger students, you may wish to use the reproducible master on page 31.

Name	Physical Description
Feelings	**Character Traits**

3. Before reading the story, it may be helpful to relate aspects of Character Four Square to yourself. You may want to invite students to share their ideas, so you can help them distinguish between feelings and traits.

4. Explain the procedure and the words in each quadrant. You might say the following.

> Look at the words in each of these squares. Let's talk about what these words mean. Stories have characters. They can be people or animals. After I read *The Bird, the Frog, and the Light* (Avi, 1994), we will write the name of a character here. [Point to the appropriate square in each case.] In the next square, we will list words that tell what the character looks like—what I would see if I looked with my eyes. As I read, think of some feelings the character may have. We'll want to list those here. Then talk about the traits characters can have, such as honesty.

5. After reading the story, invite students to decide which character to write in the top left quadrant. Then add any physical description students can remember from the story. You may want to read certain parts of the story again to help students recall descriptions, feelings, and traits. Systematically complete the Character Four Square, offering clarification as needed. Below is a completed example for *The Bird, the Frog, and the Light*.

Name Frog	Physical Description yellow toes big green bulging wore a crown
Feelings important sad	Character Traits bossy proud mean impatient

6. Be sure to help students understand that most feelings and traits must be inferred from what the characters say and do. Below is an example.

    Mr. Lane: You did a great job describing how Frog looked by using the pictures and what the author actually said. But when we list feelings and traits, the author may not actually say the words. We have to infer or guess what the author might have in mind from the story. Who has an idea for a word that describes Frog's character? Be sure and tell why you think so. What is your evidence?

    Cherrith: I think Frog was bossy. He ordered Bird around.

    Corey: Frog was also proud. The story said he puffed himself up. The picture also showed him puffed up.

    Max: I think being puffed up was Frog's way to feel important. You can tell that Frog wanted to feel important from the way he acted.

    Josh: Frog was also mean. I didn't like the way he talked to Bird. He ordered Bird around, and Mr. Lane sounded mean when he read that part of the story.

    Mr. Lane: You have shared some appropriate traits and feelings for Frog. I especially liked how you used your ideas along with the story to come up with words.

7. If the story or selection has other characters, they may be discussed using another Character Four Square. For example, Character Four Square can be completed for Bird and Light in *The Bird, the Frog, and the Light*.

8. When students understand the strategy, have them work in small groups, with partners, or individually. Young students may draw pictures for the character and some of the feelings and descriptions. Reproducible masters can be found on pages 30 and 31.

Reference

Avi. (1994). *The Bird, the Frog, and the Light*. New York: Overland Books.

Name _____ Date _____

 # Character Four Square

Character's Name	Physical Description
Feelings	**Character Traits**

Character Four Square

My character's name	Words that tell how my character looks
Feelings my character shows or has	**A drawing of my character showing traits**

Concept Circles

FOCUS		TEXT		WHEN			WHY									HOW			
Comprehension	Vocabulary	Narrative	Informational	Before Reading	During Reading	After Reading	Predicting	Connecting	Questioning	Using Text Structure	Visualizing	Inferring	Summarizing	Synthesizing	Determining Importance	Individual	Partner	Small Group	Whole Group
•			•			•						•		•	•	•	•		

DESCRIPTION

Concept Circles (Vacca & Vacca, 2002) provide opportunities for students to think about how words and their related concepts are connected. Concept Circles are intriguing to students because they classify words in a visual way. This strategy is often viewed by students as "fun," while providing an opportunity for them to extend their understanding of words and terms they are learning.

There are three ways to work with Concept Circles. The first way has students view a completed circle containing two to four words or phrases and then identify the concept represented by the words or phrases in the circle. In a second pattern, one or two of the segments of the circle are left empty, and students are invited to add words and/or pictures that fit the concept. Students may also be asked to name the concept. The third way of using Concept Circles is to ask students to identify a word or phrase in the circle that does not belong. Students can also be asked to replace the word or phrase that doesn't belong with one that fits the overall concept. All of the ways of working with Concept Circles involve students in thinking about how words relate to each other and how they relate to a superordinate concept. Concept Circles can serve as a quick and meaningful review of ideas and also as a way to help students begin to think about how words and concepts are alike or different.

Teaching Goals

1. To have students connect vocabulary to a concept or idea.
2. To encourage students to synthesize vocabulary knowledge to make distinctions among words related to a concept.
3. To help students classify words or make connections among words.

Procedure

1. Select the type of Concept Circle you wish to introduce to your students. Make a transparency of the appropriate reproducible master (see pages 37–39) and display it on an overhead projector. Tell students that this type of graphic can help them think about the meanings of some of the words they are learning and how the words may be connected.

2. Model the use of Concept Circles by choosing well-understood concepts and inviting the class to participate in completing the circles with you. For example, the words in the circle might be *Brown Bear, Charlotte's Web, A House of Tailors,* and *Clifford, The Big Red Dog.* Ask students, "What is the big idea that includes all of these words?"

    Students should offer ideas such as "books" or "names of books in our classroom library." Write the category they select on the line above the circle and help students understand that the category includes all the words in the circle.

3. After students have become familiar with the first way of using Concept Circles, choose to model a circle where the words included might be *flag, desk,* and *chalkboard* and one segment is left blank. Ask, "How are these words connected?" Students might say, "They are things in our classroom." Write the response on the line at the top of the transparency. Ask, "What word could you add to our circle that fits our title?" Students might suggest *clock, book shelves,* or *tables.* Choose one and write it in the blank section of the circle.

4. After students have become familiar with the first two uses of Concept Circles, show students a completed circle in which one of the words included in the circle does not fit the concept. Have students read the words in this circle. Then say, "One of the words doesn't belong. Can you tell me which one doesn't belong and why you think so?"

    An example might be *banana, pear, apple, candy bar.* After students identify *candy bar* as the word that doesn't fit, cross out the word or shade in that section of the circle on the transparency with an overhead marking pen. Then ask students to identify the concept *fruit* and ask them to suggest a replacement for *candy bar* that does fit the concept. Students might suggest *orange, peach,* or *plum.* Write the new word in the circle.

5. After modeling the strategy, give students an opportunity to complete Concept Circles independently. You may want to invite students to work individually or in pairs to complete Concept Circle activities. Have them use circles you have developed or give students blank copies of the appropriate reproducible master from pages 37–39. Ask them to create circles using words from a lesson or unit of study that is ongoing in your classroom.

6. When the circles are completed, have students share some of their ideas or transfer them to a transparency and present them to the rest of the class. Their peers will enjoy matching wits with the circles' creators by guessing the categories, suggesting other words that might relate to the category, or reviewing the words that don't "fit" those in the circle.

Reference

Vacca, R. T., & Vacca, J. L. (2002). *Content area reading: Literacy and learning across the curriculum* (7th ed.). Boston: Allyn and Bacon.

Concept Circles

➥ **DIRECTIONS**
1. Read the words in each circle.
2. Think of a word or phrase that tells how they are all alike.
3. Write that word or phrase on the line above the circle.

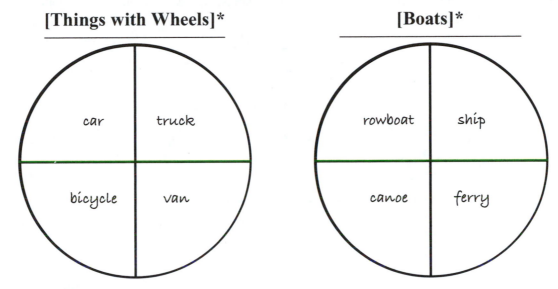

[Things with Wheels]*

car | truck

bicycle | van

[Boats]*

rowboat | ship

canoe | ferry

➥ **DIRECTIONS**
1. Read the words in each circle.
2. Think of a word or phrase that tells how they are all alike.
3. Write that word or phrase on the line above the circle.
4. Now add a word or phrase to the circle that fits with the others.

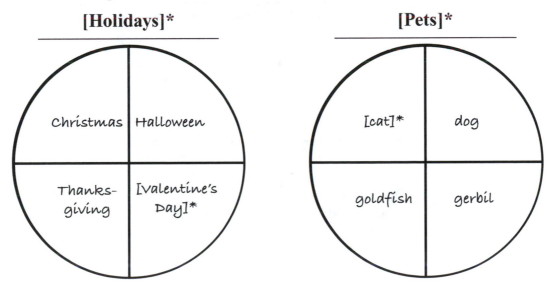

[Holidays]*

Christmas | Halloween

Thanks-giving | [Valentine's Day]*

[Pets]*

[cat]* | dog

goldfish | gerbil

*Brackets [ ] indicate possible student responses.

Concept Circles

⇒ **DIRECTIONS**

1. Read the words in each circle. One of them doesn't belong. Draw a line through it.
2. Think of a word or phrase that tells how the other words are alike. Write that word or phrase on the line above the circle.
3. Replace the word you have crossed out with a word or phrase that *does* belong with the others in the circle. Write it in the circle.

[Feeling Sad]*

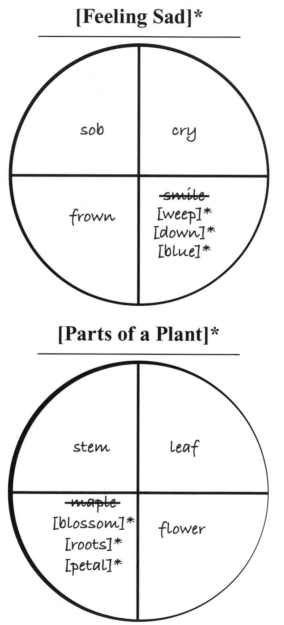

[Parts of a Plant]*

*Brackets [ ] indicate possible student responses.

Name _____ Date _____

 **Concept Circles**

_____
(topic)

➡ **DIRECTIONS**

1. Read the words in each circle.
2. Think of a word or phrase that tells how they are all alike.
3. Write that word or phrase on the line above the circle.

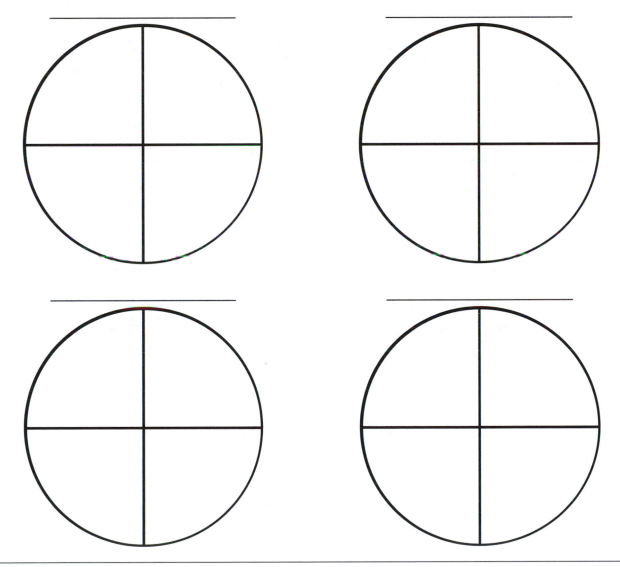

 # Concept Circles

_____
(topic)

➡ **DIRECTIONS**

1. Read the words in each circle.
2. Think of a word or phrase that tells how they are all alike.
3. Write that word or phrase on the line above the circle.
4. Think of a word or phrase that fits with the others in the circle.
5. Write your word or phrase in the circle.

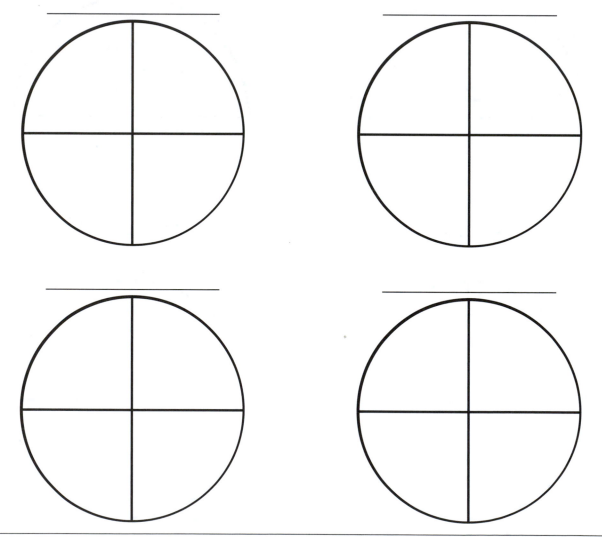

Based on Vacca, R.T., & Vacca, J.L. (2002). *Content area reading: Literacy and learning across the curriculum* (7th ed.). Boston: Allyn and Bacon.

Name _____ Date _____

 **Concept Circles**

_____
(topic)

⇒ **DIRECTIONS**
1. Read the words in each circle. One of them **doesn't** belong. Draw a line through it.
2. Think of a word or phrase that tells how the words are alike. Write that word or phrase on the line above the circle.
3. Replace the word you have crossed out with a word or phrase that *does* belong with the others in the circle. Write it in the circle.

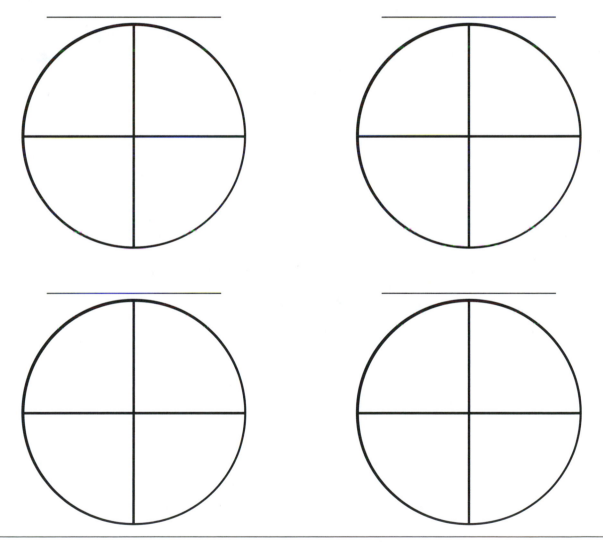

Based on Vacca, R. T., & Vacca, J. L. (2002). *Content area reading: Literacy and learning across the curriculum* (7th ed.). Boston: Allyn and Bacon.

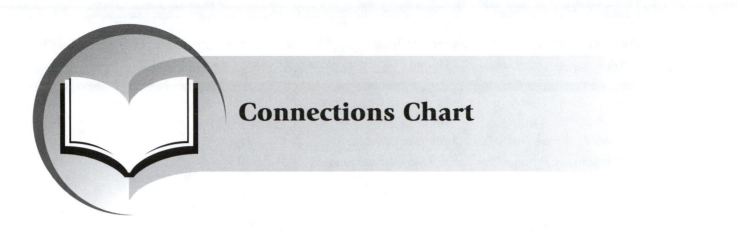

Connections Chart

FOCUS		TEXT		WHEN			WHY									HOW			
Comprehension	Vocabulary	Narrative	Informational	Before Reading	During Reading	After Reading	Predicting	Connecting	Questioning	Using Text Structure	Visualizing	Inferring	Summarizing	Synthesizing	Determining Importance	Individual	Partner	Small Group	Whole Group
•		•	•		•	•	•	•							•	•	•	•	•

DESCRIPTION

A Connections Chart helps students make connections during and after reading. Students make connections to themselves, other texts, and the world at large. Making connections is an internal reading process used by good readers that can be directly taught (Hartman, 1995).

Teaching Goals

1. To help students see ways to connect current reading to their lives, other texts, and the world.
2. To provide students with practice in making connections during and after reading.

Procedure

1. Tell students that when they read they should make connections to their lives, other books they have read, and other things they know. Provide an example of a book you've read and the things that came to your mind as in the example that follows.

   Last night I finished reading the book *Flight to Freedom* by Ana Veciana-Suarez (2002) which was a book about a girl named Yara and how her family came to the United States from Cuba. As I read the book, I thought about some of my own personal experiences that connected with the book.

   • My great-grandfather came to the United States from Sweden in the hold of a huge ship. He was sick the entire way across the Atlantic Ocean.

- I've met many people who came from Cuba.
- I know many immigrants to the United States who came from other countries.

While I was reading *Flight to Freedom,* I also thought about other books I had read about children coming to a new country or that took place in Cuba. Some of the books I thought about were the following.

- *Friends From the Other Side: Amigos del otro lado*
- *A Movie in my Pillow: Una película en mi almohada*
- *My Diary from Here to There: Mi diario de aquí hasta allá*
- *Mama does the Mambo*

I also made all sorts of connections to other things I knew about students immigrating, Cuba, and Latin America as I read. Some of the many connections I made follow.

- Cuba is a small island south of Florida.
- There are many people from Cuba who live in our area.
- Children who immigrate to a new culture need extra support in learning procedures and rules.
- Learning a new language can take many months or even years.

2. Discuss with students reasons why making connections can help them become better readers as in the following example.

When you read, you should try to make a variety of connections to things you know. When you make these connections, you are expanding the way you are thinking about your reading. You know that good readers understand what they are reading. In order to understand something new, it helps to connect new information with things you already know. That's why making connections is an important strategy for you.

3. Explain to students that when they hear stories or read they also make connections to things they know, but these connections can be made so quickly that they do not remember them. Tell students that using a Connections Chart can help them remember the connections they make.

4. Demonstrate making connections by selecting a story or a passage with which students are unfamiliar or use the example that follows from *Hey, Little Ant* (Hoose & Hoose, 1998). Duplicate and distribute the Connections Chart on page 44 to use to demonstrate the strategy.

5. Show students the title of the story and ask students what they think the story will be about. For example, a conversation before reading *Hey, Little Ant* could be something like the following.

Teacher: Write the title of the story on the top of the Connections Chart. Then look at the front cover and think about the title. What do you think this story will be about?

Student: The picture shows a little ant looking at a boy's glasses. The ant looks scared. Maybe the story will be about a boy and his pet ant.

Teacher: That's a wonderful prediction. Now I want all of you to make connections to your lives, books you've read, and other things so that you can make more predictions.

6. Read the story to students or have them read the story in pairs. Stop halfway through the story and have students think about the connections they could make to the story. Begin by asking students to think of connections to their lives and have them write these ideas in the left-hand column of the Connections Chart. Then have students make connections to other books and to other knowledge they have about ants. Write some of the connections on the board as in the example that follows.

Connections to our lives
- There are lots of ants on the sidewalk in front of school.
- Ants covered a piece of bread I dropped during a picnic.

Connections to other books
- Science book
- Book on ants from the library

Connections to the world
- Some ants bite.
- Ants are small but there are different sizes of ants.

7. Encourage students to share the connections they have made with other students in the class. Explain to students that when they hear about connections others have made they can also expand their knowledge.

8. Write the connections students made on the Connections Chart or have students write their own connections on individual charts.

9. Demonstrate the Connections Chart several times using a variety of different books. As students become more proficient with making connections, encourage them to use the Connections Charts on pages 44–50 when they read independently.

10. Extend students' learning by adapting the Connections Chart (page 45). See the example below.

FROM THE STORY	CONNECTION (CIRCLE)	WHAT I LEARNED FROM THIS CONNECTION
In <u>Old Yeller</u>, Travis has to keep the farm going while his father is away for several months.	Self (Text) World In <u>Sign of the Beaver</u>, Matt stays alone while his father returns East for the rest of the family.	The two boys both have to learn many new things to manage on their own.

References

Anzaldua, G. (1993). *Friends from the other side: Amigos del otro lado.* San Francisco: Children's Book Press.

Argueta, J. (2001). *A movie in my pillow: Una película en mi almohada.* San Francisco: Children's Book Press.

Hartman, D. K. (1995). Eight readers reading: The intertextual links of proficient readers reading multiple passages. *Reading Research Quarterly, 30,* 520–561.

Hoose, P., & Hoose, H. (1998). *Hey, little ant.* New York: Scholastic.

Leiner, K. (2001). *Mama does the mambo.* New York: Hyperion Books.

Pérez, A. I. (2002). *My diary from here to there: Mi diario de aquí hasta allá.* San Francisco: Children's Book Press.

Veciana-Suarez, A. (2002). *Flight to freedom.* New York: Orchard.

Name _____ Date _____

Title _____

 **Connections Chart**

CONNECTIONS TO SELF	CONNECTIONS TO OTHER TEXTS	CONNECTIONS TO THE WORLD

Name _____ Date _____

Title _____

Connections Chart

FROM THE STORY	CONNECTION (CIRCLE)	WHAT I LEARNED FROM THIS CONNECTION
	Self Text World	
	Self Text World	
	Self Text World	

Name _____

Title _____

Date _____

Connections Chart

➡ DIRECTIONS
Fill in the "From the Story" box for each connection. Then fill in the connections boxes that fit the connections you make.

FROM THE STORY	CONNECTIONS TO SELF	CONNECTIONS TO TEXTS	CONNECTIONS TO THE WORLD

Name _____ Date _____

Book Title _____

 # Connections Chart

WHAT I READ	WAYS IT'S LIKE ME

Name _____ Date _____

Book Title _____

 **Connections Chart**

WHAT I READ	WAYS IT'S LIKE ME OR SOMEONE I KNOW

Name _____ Date _____

Book Title _____

 **Connections Chart**

THIS BOOK SAID . . .	THIS BOOK REMINDED ME OF . . .

Name _____ Date _____

Book Title _____

Connections Chart

WHAT IT SAID . . .	SOMETHING ELSE I KNOW . . .

Directed Reading-Thinking Activity (DR-TA)
Directed Listening-Thinking Activity (DL-TA)

FOCUS		TEXT		WHEN			WHY									HOW			
Comprehension	Vocabulary	Narrative	Informational	Before Reading	During Reading	After Reading	Predicting	Connecting	Questioning	Using Text Structure	Visualizing	Inferring	Summarizing	Synthesizing	Determining Importance	Individual	Partner	Small Group	Whole Group
•		•		•	•	•	•	•	•			•						•	

DESCRIPTION

The Directed Reading-Thinking Activity (DR-TA) (Stauffer, 1975) and its companion strategy, the Directed Listening-Thinking Activity (DL-TA) (Richek, 1987), help students become critical readers or listeners as they make and check predictions about the content of a text. While the DR-TA and DL-TA can be used with informational text, they are most often introduced and used with narrative text. The DR-TA and DL-TA help students set purposes for reading or listening, understand information, actively read or listen to a text, and check the accuracy of predictions made about its content.

Teaching Goals

1. To help students become actively involved in reading a selection or listening to a selection.
2. To encourage students to make predictions and ask questions prior to and during reading and listening.
3. To encourage students to set purposes for reading and listening.

Procedure

1. Select a book or story that can elicit rich predictions. A selection with a well-defined plot and events, as well as a surprise ending, are often useful in introducing this strategy.
2. Prior to introducing the book or story to students, choose a small number of stopping points in the text. These points could be related to major events in the story or those that will encourage reflection and conjecture about the meaning of the text.

3. Invite students to look at the title or cover of the reading material and answer the following question.

    What do you think this book (or story) is going to be about?

    Provide opportunities for several students to respond. You may want to record their predictions on the board or on chart paper. As students offer predictions, follow each by asking, "Why?" or "What makes you think so?" Allow several students to make predictions and explain their thinking.

4. In order to involve all students in making predictions and setting purposes for reading or listening, ask those students who have not actively made predictions to raise their hands indicating which prediction they agree with. You might say the following.

    Jenny, we have three predictions written on the board. Which one do you think is the best prediction of what our story is going to be about?

5. In some situations you might use the following options. Read each prediction aloud and have students raise their hands to indicate their choice. For younger students, after three or four predictions are given, have the children who contributed the predictions move to different corners of the room. Have the remaining students go and stand with the person whose prediction they agree with. Repeat this process after each stopping point in the selection.

6. When several predictions have been made, ask students to read or listen until a predetermined stopping point in the text has been reached. Then ask students to reconsider their predictions.

    Were your predictions correct? Why or why not? [Invite several students to explain their thinking.]

7. When several of the predictions have been discussed, ask students if they wish to change their predictions and/or to make new ones. Again, ask them to explain their reasoning.

8. Continue with the prediction, read (or listen), and prove cycle until enough information has been presented for the ideas to begin to converge. At this point, finish the story.

9. At the completion of the story, follow up with reading (or listening) response activities, word study, meaningful rereading, or concept development. Reproducible masters on pages 53–55 are for use in a reading or listening center in the classroom.

References

Richek, M. A. (1987). DR-TA: 5 variations that facilitate independence in reading narratives. *Journal of Reading, 30,* 632–636.

Stauffer, R. E. (1975). *Directing the reading-thinking process.* New York: Harper & Row.

Thinking about My Reading or Listening

Before you read or listen, draw a picture showing what you think the story will be about.

Were you right? Why or why not? Change your picture or draw a new one showing your ideas about the story now.

Jerry L. Johns, Susan Davis Lenski, and Roberta L. Berglund. *Comprehension and Vocabulary Strategies for the Elementary Grades* (2nd ed.). Copyright © 2006 by Kendall/Hunt Publishing Company (1-800-247-3458, ext. 4). May be reproduced for noncommercial educational purposes within the guidelines noted on the copyright page.

It is important to keep thinking as you read or listen. Remember to ask yourself these questions.

What is this going to be about?

What makes me think so?

Was I right? Why or why not?

How could I change my ideas to match what I know so far?

What will happen next?

What makes me think so?

Name _____ Date _____

 # Thinking about My Reading or Listening

⇒ DIRECTIONS

Before you read or listen, make a prediction about what will happen. Explain why you think as you do. After reading or listening, evaluate your prediction.

Prediction 1 _____

_____

Why I think so _____

_____

Now I think _____

_____

Prediction 2 _____

_____

Why I think so _____

_____

Now I think _____

_____

Info Boxes

FOCUS		TEXT		WHEN			WHY									HOW			
Comprehension	Vocabulary	Narrative	Informational	Before Reading	During Reading	After Reading	Predicting	Connecting	Questioning	Using Text Structure	Visualizing	Inferring	Summarizing	Synthesizing	Determining Importance	Individual	Partner	Small Group	Whole Group
•	•	•				•							•		•	•	•	•	•

DESCRIPTION

Info Boxes (adapted from Allen, 2000; Hoyt, 1999) provide a way for students to record information about a topic after reading, listening, or viewing. The completed boxes can be used as a basis for discussion, for creating summaries, or as a source of information for use in more extensive writing projects. They also can be used as study guides for test preparation. Beers (2003) suggests using this strategy with narrative text to record adjectives that describe characters. Different colored pens or pencils are used for each character. When the grid is completed, it can be used to compare and contrast each of the characters.

Teaching Goals

1. To invite students to recall their knowledge about a topic.
2. To encourage students to determine the most important ideas with a rationale for their choices.
3. To help students organize and use information.

Procedure

1. Create a grid containing one or more letters of the alphabet in each box of the grid or use one provided on pages 60–63.
2. Write the topic or title at the top of the grid.
3. Provide copies of the grid to students.

4. After the grid is distributed, you might say the following.

    We have been reading and learning about Ancient Greece. Think about the information you have learned and use the grid to record it. Try to record one or more ideas in each box of the grid. Each of the ideas must start with the letter or one of the letters of the alphabet that are written in the grid.

5. When students have completed the task, either individually or with a partner, say the following.

    Look at your grid of information. Compare your grid with another person or group of students. Add additional ideas to your grid. When you have finished, review the information in your grid. Decide which information is the most important and circle it.

6. When students have determined the most important information, encourage them to use the information to write a summary or use the ideas for creating a longer piece of writing on the topic. The circled ideas can become the major points or paragraphs of the piece. Info Boxes are also excellent for use in chapter reviews and as a study aid.

References

Allen, J. (2000). *Yellow brick roads: Shared and guided paths to independent reading 4–12.* Portland, ME: Stenhouse.

Beers, K. (2003). *When kids can't read what teachers can do: A guide for teachers 6–12.* Portsmouth, NH: Heinemann.

Hoyt, L. (1999). *Revisit, reflect, retell: Strategies for improving reading comprehension.* Portsmouth, NH: Heinemann.

Info Boxes

Name __Tasia__   Date __October 10__

Title/Subject __Icebergs__

A Antarctica Alaska	B Break off	C Cause shipwrecks	D Damage ships
E	F Frozen Float Form in warm weather	G	H Heavy-most is under water
I Ice breaks and crashes into sea	J	K	L Large pieces of ice

 **Info Boxes**

Name _____ Date _____

Title/Subject _____

A	B	C	D
E	F	G	H
I	J	K	L
M	N	O	P
Q	R	S	T
U	V	W	XYZ

Info Boxes

Name _____ Date _____

Title/Subject _____

AB	CD	EF	GH
IJ	KL	MN	OP
QRS	TU	VW	XYZ

 **Info Boxes**

Name _____ Date _____

Title/Subject _____

AB	CD	EF	GH
IJ	KL	MN	OP
QR	ST	UV	WXYZ

Info Boxes

Name _____ Date _____

Title/Subject _____

AB	CD	EF	GH
IJ	KL	MN	OP
QRS	TU	VW	XYZ

Summary: _____

_____

_____

_____

_____

_____

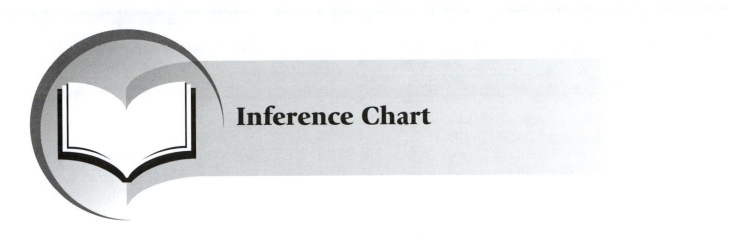

Inference Chart

FOCUS		TEXT		WHEN			WHY									HOW			
Comprehension	Vocabulary	Narrative	Informational	Before Reading	During Reading	After Reading	Predicting	Connecting	Questioning	Using Text Structure	Visualizing	Inferring	Summarizing	Synthesizing	Determining Importance	Individual	Partner	Small Group	Whole Group
•		•			•	•		•				•				•	•	•	•

DESCRIPTION

An Inference Chart is a way for students to make inferences by connecting clues or details they read in narrative text to their own experiences. Making inferences is a strategy readers use to "read between the lines." Writers do not always specify the links between details and events in stories; they expect readers to do that. Some students, though, need explicit instruction and practice in learning how to make inferences. An Inference Chart can help students with this strategy.

Teaching Goals

1. To help students make inferences from the details or clues they learn in narrative texts.
2. To help students connect their knowledge and experiences with story details or clues.
3. To provide students with opportunities to make inferences and to hear the inferences of others.

Procedure

1. Tell students that they will be practicing a strategy called building inferences as they read. Write the term "inferences" on the board. Explain to students that they already build inferences as they read but that you will help them with this strategy.

2. Discuss "making inferences" with students. Tell students that inferences are the guesses that readers make as they read text. Explain to students that building inferences is also known as "reading between the lines." Generate a discussion about times students have "read between the lines" in conversations or other aspects of life. You might use the following example.

   We were driving past my favorite ice cream store the other day. My husband knew that I had not had any ice cream that week and that I had had a busy day. He slowed the car before we got to the store and said, "Look there's a parking spot right in front of the ice cream store. Do you want to stop?"

3. Discuss with students what clues were offered in this story. You might mention that they had learned that my husband knew that I loved ice cream, that I had not had ice cream that week, and that the opportunity was available to stop. Using experience about how people act, discuss the inferences you could build about this anecdote. For example, you could build the inference that we would get ice cream. Elicit other logical inferences discussing how students used clues from the story to build the inferences.

4. Ask students why they think that inferences are made, not merely known. Reinforce the idea that inferences are personal and that they will vary with each individual and in each reading situation. There can also be inferences that we agree on. Remind students that inferences should, however, be built using text information.

5. Duplicate and distribute one of the Inference Charts that follow on pages 68–69. Point out the areas on the chart that students will use: the details or clues from the story, experiences, and inferences. Tell students that you will use the Inference Chart together with an example.

6. Select a story that provides opportunities for students to build inferences such as *América Is Her Name* by Luis J. Rodríguez (2001). This story is based on the author's work with Mexican immigrants in Chicago.

7. Read the story with students or have them read it in small groups. Ask students to volunteer the kinds of details they learned in the story. Some of the possibilities follow.

   América was a Mixteca Indian girl from Oaxaca, Mexico.

   América is nine years old.

   She lives with her extended family.

   Her father works in a factory.

   She meets lots of people on her way to school.

   She sees a boy shoot a gun at a gang member on her way to school.

   In school, her teacher yells at the students.

   América daydreams of Mexico during class.

   América hears her teacher call her "an illegal."

   América likes reciting and writing poetry.

   A poet from Puerto Rico comes to her class.

   América begins writing poetry.

8. Have students select ideas from the story to write in the first column of the Inference Chart. Ask students to then write one of their personal experiences in the next column that relates to the story idea. Illustrate how to connect story details with personal experiences to build inferences as follows.

   I decided to write this important detail from the story.

   Detail: América daydreams of Mexico during class.

   When I thought about my own experiences that could help me understand how América was feeling, I remembered a situation where I was in Italy sitting in a class where I was learning how to cook. I couldn't understand the teacher very well, and I was thinking about my own home and my own kitchen. I was very homesick and unhappy. That personal experience could help me so I'll write it on the chart.

Personal Experience: Cooking in Italy

To build inferences, I need to connect what happens in the story with my own experiences so I can read between the lines. The story doesn't say that América is homesick, but I infer that she is. I build that inference from the details of the story and my own experience. I'll write the inference in the third column.

Inference: América is homesick.

9. Write other details from the story on the Inference Chart. Have students generate their own experiences that build on the story ideas. Discuss the students' experiences and talk about the inferences they can draw from the experiences.

10. Ask students to list two or three additional ideas from the story to write on their Inference Chart, write their own experiences, and make inferences. Reassure students that each person's experiences and inferences could be different.

11. Remind students when they read independently to use story details and clues to connect with their experiences to make inferences.

Reference
Rodríguez, L. J. (2001). *América is her name.* Willimantic, CT: Curbstone Press.

Name _____ Date _____

Title _____

 **Inference Chart**

CLUES OR DETAILS FROM STORY	MY EXPERIENCES	MY INFERENCE

Name _____ Date _____

Title _____

Inference Chart

CLUES	MY LIFE	WHAT I THINK

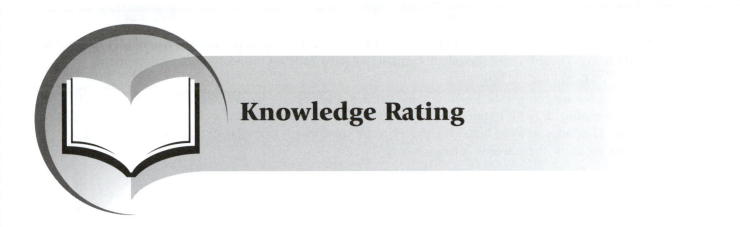

Knowledge Rating

FOCUS		TEXT		WHEN			WHY									HOW			
Comprehension	Vocabulary	Narrative	Informational	Before Reading	During Reading	After Reading	Predicting	Connecting	Questioning	Using Text Structure	Visualizing	Inferring	Summarizing	Synthesizing	Determining Importance	Individual	Partner	Small Group	Whole Group
•	•	•	•	•		•	•		•							•			

DESCRIPTION

Knowledge Rating (Blachowicz, 1986; Blachowicz & Fisher, 2006) is a strategy that helps students become aware of the words in a text prior to reading it. The strategy helps students activate their prior knowledge about a topic and encourages them to develop mental questions and predictions about what is to be read. Students can also return to the Knowledge Rating sheet after reading and, using a different color pen or pencil, rate their knowledge of the words again.

Teaching Goals

1. To create student interest in reading a selection.
2. To help students preview new and familiar vocabulary in a reading selection or unit of study.
3. To help students activate prior knowledge and develop a purpose for reading.

Procedure

1. Carefully select key vocabulary words from the selection to be read. Mix words that are new to the students with those that may be familiar to them.
2. Write these words on the reproducible master on page 74, duplicate it, and distribute it to students.

3. Model how to use the sheet by listing the words on an overhead transparency created from the How Well Do I Know These Words? reproducible master on page 74 or on the board with appropriate headings. You might say the following.

> This week we are going to be learning about *caribou*. I have put some words on the board that will be in our reading. It helps to think about what we know about some of the words in our book before we read. This helps us to be better readers. Here are some words from the text. Let's see how well we think we know these words before we read.

4. Show students the first word, *caribou,* and say the following.

> I need to think about how much I already know about *caribou*. I definitely have heard the word before, and I know what it means. Therefore, I am going to put an "x" in the box under the *Know It Well* column. A *caribou* is a large reindeer.

> Now let's look at another word from our reading. This one is *tundra*. Let's see, I know I have seen and heard it before. So I think I will put my "x" under *Think I Know It*. I think I know what this word means, but I'll need to read and find out if I am right.

5. Display the next word and invite a student to come to the board or overhead projector and show where he or she would put an "x" indicating his or her familiarity with the word. Invite the student to explain why he or she marked the word in a particular column.

6. When students appear to be comfortable with the How Well Do I Know These Words? grid, distribute the grid to students and ask them to complete the grid independently. A sample completed grid is shown on page 73.

7. When students have finished, review the words and ask students who marked an "x" in the *Know It Well* column to explain what they know about the words.

8. Finally, invite students to make predictions about the content of the lesson. After the lesson, the words can be revisited to assess knowledge gained about the words.

References

Blachowicz, C. L. Z. (1986). Making connections: Alternatives to the vocabulary notebook. *Journal of Reading, 29,* 643–649.

Blachowicz, C., & Fisher, P. (2006). *Teaching vocabulary in all classrooms* (3rd ed.). Upper Saddle River, NJ: Merrill Prentice Hall.

How Well Do I Know These Words?

➥ DIRECTIONS

Here are some words from your reading. Before you read, put an "x" in the box that tells how well you think you know each word.

WORD	1 KNOW IT WELL	2 THINK I KNOW IT	3 DON'T KNOW IT
caribou	x		
reindeer	x		
tundra		x	
migrate		x	
lichen			x
graze		x	
marsh			x
mosquitoes	x		

Jerry L. Johns, Susan Davis Lenski, and Roberta L. Berglund. *Comprehension and Vocabulary Strategies for the Elementary Grades* (2nd ed.). Copyright © 2006 by Kendall/Hunt Publishing Company (1-800-247-3458, ext. 4). May be reproduced for noncommercial educational purposes within the guidelines noted on the copyright page.

Name _____ Date _____

 # How Well Do I Know These Words?

⇒ **DIRECTIONS**

Here are some words from your reading. Before you read, put an "x" in the box that tells how well you think you know each word.

WORD	1 KNOW IT WELL	2 THINK I KNOW IT	3 DON'T KNOW IT

Based on Blachowicz, C. L. Z. (1986). Making connections: Alternatives to the vocabulary notebook. *Journal of Reading, 29,* 643–649 and Blachowicz, C., & Fisher, P. (2006). *Teaching vocabulary in all classrooms* (3rd ed.). Upper Saddle River, NJ: Merrill Prentice Hall.

Name _____ Date _____

Rate Your Vocabulary Knowledge

➟ DIRECTIONS

Look at the words below. Then rate your knowledge of each word by putting an "x" in the box that best describes your knowledge.

WORD	I KNOW IT WELL.	I'M PRETTY SURE I KNOW IT.	I HAVE HEARD IT, BUT I DON'T KNOW WHAT IT MEANS.	I HAVE NEVER SEEN IT BEFORE.

Based on Blachowicz, C. L. Z. (1986). Making connections: Alternatives to the vocabulary notebook. *Journal of Reading, 29,* 643–649 and Blachowicz, C., & Fisher, P. (2006). *Teaching vocabulary in all classrooms* (3rd ed.). Upper Saddle River, NJ: Merrill Prentice Hall.

Name _____ Date _____

 # Knowledge Rating Scale

⇒ DIRECTIONS

Read the words below. Rate your knowledge of the words by checking the appropriate column beside each word.

WORD	KNOW IT WELL	HAVE SEEN IT	HAVE HEARD IT	NO CLUE
1. _____	____	____	____	____
2. _____	____	____	____	____
3. _____	____	____	____	____
4. _____	____	____	____	____
5. _____	____	____	____	____
6. _____	____	____	____	____
7. _____	____	____	____	____
8. _____	____	____	____	____
9. _____	____	____	____	____
10. _____	____	____	____	____

Based on Blachowicz, C. L. Z. (1986). Making connections: Alternatives to the vocabulary notebook. *Journal of Reading, 29,* 643–649 and Blachowicz, C., & Fisher, P. (2006). *Teaching vocabulary in all classrooms* (3rd ed.). Upper Saddle River, NJ: Merrill Prentice Hall.

Name _____ Date _____

Rate Your Knowledge

➳ **DIRECTIONS**

1. Rate in pencil before reading.   2. Read.   3. Rate again in pen or marker.

VOCABULARY WORD	4 I CAN DEFINE IT.	3 I CAN USE IT IN A SENTENCE.	2 I HAVE HEARD OF IT.	1 I HAVE NO IDEA.
1.				
2.				
3.				
4.				
5.				
6.				
7.				
8.				
9.				
10.				
11.				
12.				

What new words did you learn today?

_____

_____

Name _____ Date _____

Knowledge Rating Before, During, and After Reading

Use these symbols: + I know it.   − I don't know it.   ? I'm not sure.

WORD	BEFORE READING *Do I Know the Word?*	AFTER READING *Do I Know the Word?*	AFTER DISCUSSION *Do I Know the Word?*	MEANING *The Meaning or Definition of the Word Is:*

K-W-L

FOCUS		TEXT		WHEN			WHY									HOW			
Comprehension	Vocabulary	Narrative	Informational	Before Reading	During Reading	After Reading	Predicting	Connecting	Questioning	Using Text Structure	Visualizing	Inferring	Summarizing	Synthesizing	Determining Importance	Individual	Partner	Small Group	Whole Group
•		•	•	•	•	•	•	•	•						•	•	•	•	•

DESCRIPTION

K-W-L (Ogle, 1986, 2002) is a strategy that provides readers with a framework for constructing meaning from text. Readers activate their prior knowledge through brainstorming (What I *K*now), define their purposes for reading by generating questions (What I *W*ant to Find Out), and monitor their reading by confirming their prior knowledge or extending their learning (What I *L*earned). The strategy can be used as a way of having the entire class brainstorm what they know about a topic before launching an investigation as well as a means of recording their learning once information is read or shared. Adaptations of K-W-L encourage students to identify possible sources of information and categorize the information. Students are also invited to identify additional questions following the reading. These questions can stimulate further research and inquiry.

Teaching Goals

1. To help students build interest in and knowledge about informational text.
2. To help students activate prior knowledge and establish purposes for reading.
3. To encourage students to monitor their reading.
4. To help students evaluate their prior knowledge.

Procedure

1. Create a K-W-L chart on the board, chart paper, or a transparency. Provide copies of the chart for each student, if you wish, using the reproducible on page 82.

2. Select a key concept from the topic being studied. For example, the topic being studied is spiders, and the key concept is black widow spiders. Brainstorm with students what they know about the concept. Record the information as it is shared under the heading, What We Know (or What We Think We Know). Encourage students to offer sources for the information shared.

3. After the brainstorming is complete, say the following to your students.

   Let's look at the information we think we know about black widow spiders. Do some of the ideas fit together? What categories of information might we be looking for as we read?

4. If students have difficulty clustering the brainstormed ideas into categories, you might say the following.

   I think one category of information might be where black widow spiders live. Another one might be what they look like. Can you think of others?

5. As students discuss the information they think they know about a topic, questions arise, especially if there is disagreement about some of the information shared. For example, some students may think that the black widow spider is the only spider that can be dangerous to humans. Other students may believe differently. This leads to the next step in the K-W-L procedure, What We Want to Find Out. You need to help students develop questions about the topic, especially if there are gaps in the knowledge that students have shared or if there are inconsistencies or contradictions.

6. Record questions on the K-W-L chart that is visible to the class and encourage students to write down their questions on their personal K-W-L charts. This step helps students set purposes for their reading.

7. Following the reading, direct students to record what they learned under the L section of the chart (What We Learned). If there are still questions that were unanswered in the reading, you may wish to create a fourth column, What We Still Need to Learn, and explore with students how they might investigate these questions.

References

Ogle, D.M. (1986). K-W-L: A teaching model that develops active reading of expository text. *The Reading Teacher, 39,* 564–570.

Ogle, D. (2002). *Coming together as readers.* Arlington Heights, IL: Skylight.

WHAT WE KNOW ABOUT BLACK WIDOW SPIDERS	WHAT WE WANT TO FIND OUT ABOUT BLACK WIDOW SPIDERS	WHAT WE LEARNED ABOUT BLACK WIDOW SPIDERS	WHAT WE STILL NEED TO LEARN ABOUT BLACK WIDOW SPIDERS
They are black. They bite. They are dangerous. People don't like them.	Where do they live? How big are they? How do they look? Can they kill people? Do people keep them as pets?	They live in deserts. They live in the United States. They are shiny. They are 1 1/2 inches long. They can live up to 3 years. They eat insects. They are dangerous to very young and very old people. Only the females are dangerous.	Are they kept as pets? How many eggs do they lay? Does the female hurt the males? Are there other kinds of widows? What should I do if I get bitten?

Name _____ Date _____

Topic _____

 **K-W-L**

WHAT I **KNOW**	WHAT I **WANT** TO KNOW	WHAT I **LEARNED**

I Expect to Find Information in These Categories

A. _____

B. _____

C. _____

D. _____

Name _____ Date _____

K-W-L-S-H

WHAT WE **KNOW**	WHAT WE **WANT** TO FIND OUT	WHAT WE **LEARNED**/ STILL NEED TO **LEARN**	**HOW** CAN WE LEARN MORE?

Categories of Information We Expect to Use

A. _____   E. _____

B. _____   F. _____

C. _____   G. _____

D. _____   H. _____

Name _____ Date _____

K-W-H-L Chart

WHAT I **KNOW**	WHAT I **WANT** TO KNOW	**HOW** I WILL FIND OUT	WHAT I **LEARNED**

Name _____ Date _____

K-W-H-L-S Chart about _____

KNOW _____)	**W**ANT _____)	**H**OW _____)
(What I Know About _____)	(What I Want to Know About _____)	(How I Can Find What I Want to Know About _____)

Jerry L. Johns, Susan Davis Lenski, and Roberta L. Berglund. *Comprehension and Vocabulary Strategies for the Elementary Grades* (2nd ed.). Copyright © 2006 by Kendall/Hunt Publishing Company (1-800-247-3458, ext. 4). May be reproduced for noncommercial educational purposes within the guidelines noted on the copyright page.

Name _____ Date _____

LEARN _____

(What I Learned About _____)

STILL _____

(What I Still Want to Know About _____)

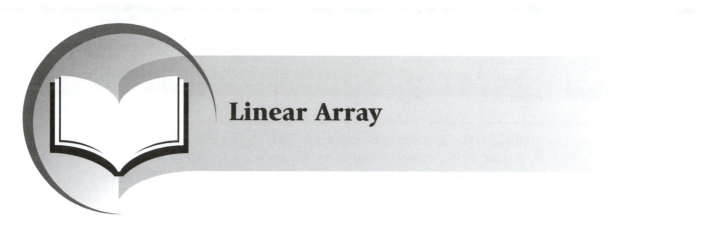

Linear Array

FOCUS		TEXT		WHEN			WHY									HOW			
Comprehension	Vocabulary	Narrative	Informational	Before Reading	During Reading	After Reading	Predicting	Connecting	Questioning	Using Text Structure	Visualizing	Inferring	Summarizing	Synthesizing	Determining Importance	Individual	Partner	Small Group	Whole Group
	•	•	•			•		•				•		•		•	•	•	•

DESCRIPTION

A Linear Array is a visual representation that depicts gradations of meaning among several related words. It can help students focus on synonyms and antonyms by arranging them along a line to visually show variations in meaning. Students can also use a Linear Array in relation to selected words in an informational passage. Linear Arrays (Allen, 1999) are similar to synonym continuums (Tompkins & Blanchfield, 2004), semantic gradients (Blachowicz & Fisher, 2006), emotion continuums (Zeigler & Johns, 2005), polar opposites, and vocabulary lines.

Teaching Goals

1. To help students expand and enlarge their vocabularies.
2. To enable students to visually show shades of meaning among similar words.
3. To help students think about the range of emotions that characters in stories can exhibit.
4. To help students clarify the meaning of related words.

Procedure

1. Draw a long line on the board. Select two words that are antonyms (like *love* and *hate*). Place one word at each end of the continuum.

   Love ———————————————————————————————————— Hate

   Select additional words that fit between these two extremes in meaning (for example, *care, indifferent, like, devotion, cherish, despise, crush, attracted, loathe, unconcerned, adore, detest,* and *dislike*). The specific words and the number of words used should depend on your students' maturity. Write the selected words on cards for possible use later in the lesson.

2. Invite students to share information about the words at the ends of the continuum. Help students realize that the words are opposite in meaning.

3. Tell students that there are some other words whose meanings are between these two very strong emotions. Invite students to offer some words that may be related to *love* and *hate* that are not as strong. Write any words students suggest on the board.

4. You might want to model an example for students. For example, you might say the following.

   I thought of the word *indifferent*. I think I would place this word at the center of the line. Its meaning is not to care much, and that seems to be between the two words.

5. Select a word written on the board (for example, *care*) and invite students to suggest where on the line the word would fit best. Guide students as necessary and provide clarification as needed. Students should understand that the meaning of *care* is not as strong as *love,* but it is stronger than *indifferent.*

6. Continue with other words and have students discuss their meanings and place the words on the continuum. Help students realize that they are thinking about words in relation to other words. Use the words on the cards for other examples if needed.

7. Encourage students to think about ways all of these words are related. For example, you can discuss how all the words from *love* to *hate* express feelings. Help students synthesize information about the group of words on the Linear Array.

8. Use a variety of continuums in subsequent lessons. For example, use weaker to stronger words or negative to positive words.

9. One variation of this strategy is to arrange the words on a ladder. For example, students could be asked to arrange a group of words (*cool, hot, torrid, lukewarm, freezing, warm, boiling, scalding, chilled,* and *frigid*) from hottest to coldest.

10. Another variation is to have students rate one or more character's emotions using a continuum. For example, students could think about Cinderella and the Prince and discuss the characters' emotions. They could then rate a particular emotion as exemplified below.

Cinderella   Fear ———————X———————————— Bravery

Prince   Fear ———————————————————X— Bravery

Reference

Allen, J. (1999). *Words, words, words: Teaching vocabulary in grades 4–12.* Portland, ME: Stenhouse.

Blachowicz, C., & Fisher, P. (2006). *Teaching vocabulary in all classrooms* (3rd ed.). Upper Saddle River, NJ: Merrill Prentice Hall.

Tompkins, G. E., & Blanchfield, C. (2004). *Teaching vocabulary.* Upper Saddle River, NJ: Merrill Prentice Hall.

Zeigler, L. L., & Johns, J. L. (2005). *Visualization: Using mental images to strengthen comprehension.* Dubuque, IA: Kendall/Hunt.

Name _____ Date _____

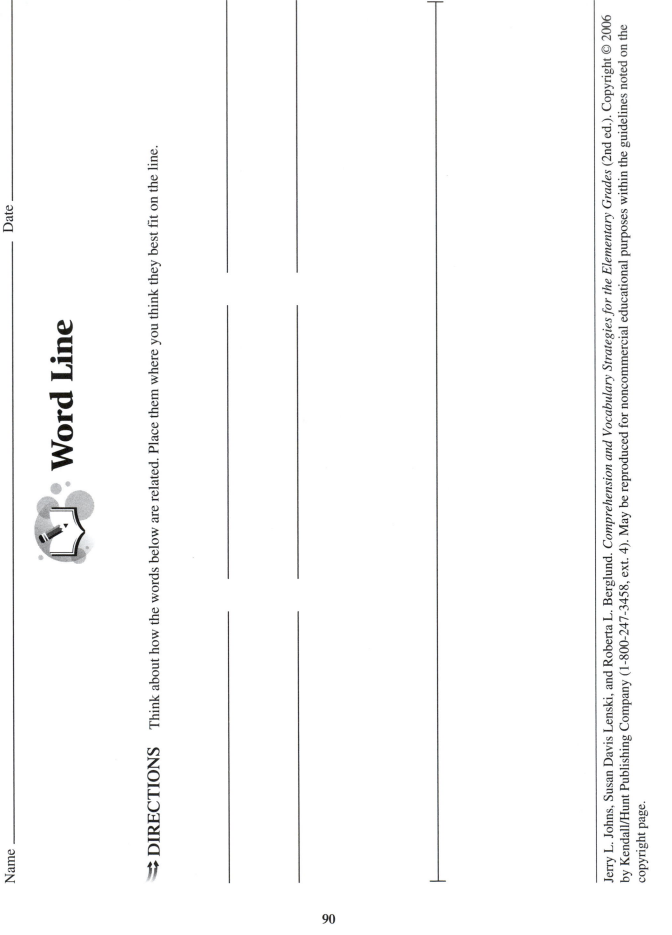

Word Line

⇉ **DIRECTIONS** Think about how the words below are related. Place them where you think they best fit on the line.

_____

_____

|_____|

Name _____ Date _____

 **Word Ladder**

➤ **DIRECTIONS**

Write the words in order on the word ladder beginning with _____ .

_____   _____   _____

_____   _____   _____

_____   _____   _____

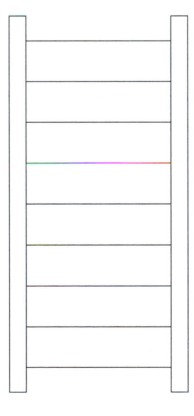

List-Group-Label

FOCUS		TEXT		WHEN			WHY									HOW			
Comprehension	Vocabulary	Narrative	Informational	Before Reading	During Reading	After Reading	Predicting	Connecting	Questioning	Using Text Structure	Visualizing	Inferring	Summarizing	Synthesizing	Determining Importance	Individual	Partner	Small Group	Whole Group
•	•		•	•		•		•							•			•	

DESCRIPTION

List-Group-Label (Taba, 1967) helps students to organize information in categorical form. By classifying and categorizing information, students become active readers and, in the process, remember new vocabulary and information.

Teaching Goals

1. To encourage students to become active readers by organizing information.
2. To help students remember new vocabulary and information from a reading selection.
3. To have students determine vocabulary that relates to a specific category.
4. To help students classify terms or concepts.

Procedure

1. Introduce a major concept or topic to students and invite them to share ideas, words, phrases, and/or experiences related to the topic. For example, *pioneers* is a topic often studied in the primary grades.

2. As students share their words and ideas, list words related to the topic on the board or an overhead transparency. For example, words related to *pioneers* might be *covered wagon, Native Americans, buckskin, hardships,* and *frontier.* Try to keep the number of responses to 20 or 25 for ease of management.

3. When the brainstormed words have been listed, read them aloud to the students. Ask students if there are ways that they think some of the words might be clustered together into categories or groups that are connected in some way. List these categories on the board or on an overhead transparency.

4. Put students into small groups and assign each group one of the categories. Give students a copy of the reproducible master on page 96. Ask students to choose words related to their category from the list on the board or overhead transparency. Ask them to think about how the words are connected to the category. It is often possible for some of the brainstormed words to become category headings. When this happens, groups might work on more than one category or a new group might be formed to focus on the new category.

5. When students have finished selecting the words they believe fit into their assigned category, invite each group to orally share the words they have included on their list with the entire class. You may wish to record these on the board or on an overhead transparency created from the reproducible master on page 97 or 98.

6. It is important for students to share reasons for their decisions. Words may be used in more than one category if the students' rationale supports such inclusion. This oral sharing stimulates students to think of the words in a variety of ways, consider their meanings, connect them, and see relationships among the words. A completed example for one group can be found on page 95.

7. If List-Group-Label is used as a prereading activity, ask students to then read or listen to the text and evaluate their decisions as they read or listen. Students may want to think about adding or deleting some words from their category list based on additional information in the lesson.

8. If List-Group-Label is used as a postreading activity, students may want to return to the groups and confirm their reasons for and accuracy of the words they included on the list for their category. They may also wish to use their completed lists to help them review and remember information in the lesson.

9. The List-Group-Label procedure can be extended over the course of several days as students acquire additional information about the topic. More words can be added to the categorized lists as students expand their knowledge and increase the connections they make between and among the words.

10. When the lists are complete, have students work individually or in pairs to write a summary of the information in one of the clusters or write a longer piece about the topic, using each one of the clusters of information as a paragraph in the longer piece.

Reference

Taba, H. (1967). *Teacher's handbook for elementary social studies.* Reading, MA: Addison-Wesley.

List-Group-Label

Write the names of the members in your group on the lines below. Then write the name of what you are studying and your group's category on the lines below your names. Next, look at the list of words. Choose the words that fit your category and write them under the column Our Words. Talk with other people in your group. Decide why each word should be in your category. Write your reason for choosing each word on the line next to the word.

Members of Our Group

Keeyan	Nigel	Dinah	Nicole

What We Are Studying

Pioneers

What They Are

Our Group's Category

Our Words	Why We Think They Fit in This Category
buffalo	They lived on the prairie and they hunted them.
rabbits	Rabbits can be used for food.
corn	We think they grew corn on their farms.
vegetables	The pioneer wives worked in gardens.
chickens	They brought chickens with them in the wagons.

95

Name _____ Date _____

🖋 List-Group-Label

⇉ DIRECTIONS

Write the names of the members in your group on the lines below. Then write the name of what you are studying and your group's category on the lines below your names. Next, look at the list of words. Choose the words that fit your category and write them under the column, Our Words. Talk with other people in your group. Decide why each word should be in your category. Write your reason for choosing each word on the line next to the word.

Members of Our Group

_____

_____

What We Are Studying

_____

Our Group's Category

_____

Our Words   Why We Think They Fit in This Category

_____   _____

_____   _____

_____   _____

_____   _____

_____   _____

Jerry L. Johns, Susan Davis Lenski, and Roberta L. Berglund. *Comprehension and Vocabulary Strategies for the Elementary Grades* (2nd ed.). Copyright © 2006 by Kendall/Hunt Publishing Company (1-800-247-3458, ext. 4). May be reproduced for noncommercial educational purposes within the guidelines noted on the copyright page.

Name _____ Date _____

List-Group-Label

_____
Topic

Category   Category

_____   _____

Words   Words

_____   _____

_____   _____

_____   _____

_____   _____

_____   _____

_____   _____

_____   _____

_____   _____

_____   _____

_____   _____

_____   _____

Name _____ Date _____

List-Group-Label

_____
Topic

Category #1 _____   Category #2 _____

Words   Words

_____   _____

_____   _____

_____   _____

_____   _____

_____   _____

Category #3 _____   Category #4 _____

Words   Words

_____   _____

_____   _____

_____   _____

_____   _____

_____   _____

Literature Circles

FOCUS		TEXT		WHEN			WHY									HOW			
Comprehension	Vocabulary	Narrative	Informational	Before Reading	During Reading	After Reading	Predicting	Connecting	Questioning	Using Text Structure	Visualizing	Inferring	Summarizing	Synthesizing	Determining Importance	Individual	Partner	Small Group	Whole Group
•	•	•		•	•	•	•	•	•		•	•	•	•	•			•	

DESCRIPTION

Literature Circles (Daniels, 1994, 2002) are small peer-led discussion groups whose members have chosen to read the same article, poem, book, or story. Literature Circles can be developed around a specific genre, a topic, an author, or a theme. Students meet regularly and participate in literate conversations centered on the text. The teacher observes group dynamics and participates briefly in each group to ask a question, redirect thinking, or expand conversation. The teacher also offers mini-lessons and models proficient reading and discussion strategies. The general procedure for days when Literature Circles are used includes the following. The teacher offers a mini-lesson related to the genre or strategy focus, and groups meet and discuss their reading. At the conclusion of the Literature Circles, the class meets and debriefs on the experience. To initiate Literature Circles, role sheets are often used; however, their use diminishes as students become more comfortable participating in open, natural conversations about text. When reading materials are finished, students share with classmates, choose new materials to read, and form new groups. Literature Circles combine two important ideas: collaborative learning and independent reading. In a Balanced Literacy framework (Fountas & Pinnell, 2000) consisting of reading aloud, shared reading, guided reading, independent reading/reading workshop, modeled writing, shared writing, interactive writing, guided writing/writing workshop, and independent writing, Literature Circles become one aspect of independent reading. Literature Circles are most often used with narrative text. To adapt them for use with informational text, see Stein and Beed (2004).

Teaching Goals

1. To encourage students to take responsibility for their own learning.
2. To help students set purposes for reading.
3. To enable students to actively construct meaning from text.
4. To encourage students to read, value, and enjoy texts.
5. To help students learn to participate in discussions.

Procedure

Week 1

1. Introduce the concept of Literature Circles to the class, if students are not familiar with them. You might say the following.

    When we read books, we often enjoy talking about our reading with someone else. Adults do this through book clubs. In book clubs, people get together and discuss their thoughts and reactions to a book they have all read. Then they choose what they will read next and schedule their next discussion. In our classroom we are going to begin the process of reading and discussing our reading in small groups. I won't be in charge of the groups when they meet; you will be. You will have a chance to choose what you will be reading and to meet and discuss your reading in small groups. We call our groups Literature Circles. This week we will be learning about some of the books we may choose to read in our Literature Circles, and we will also learn how to be effective group participants.

2. Introduce the theme or genre of the available texts, if appropriate.

3. Discuss with students how they believe they should act when they discuss their reading with others in a small group. Develop an Anchor Chart (Harvey & Goudvis, 2000) to post in the classroom for students to use as a reference.

    Suggestions for the Literature Circles Discussion Anchor Chart might include:
    - Take turns talking.
    - Keep your voice low.
    - Don't interrupt.
    - Listen to what others are saying.
    - Stay on the topic.
    - Be ready. Come to the group with the materials you need.
    - Include everyone.
    - Be polite.
    - Don't spoil the discussion by reading ahead.

4. Note that suggestions can be added to the chart as Literature Circle use grows.

5. Explain that in order to help students learn to have a good discussion about a text, they will have different jobs to do when their group meets. For the next few days, students will be learning these jobs.

6. Choose a short text to use as a read aloud. Introduce the text and explain that one of the jobs that students will be doing in their Literature Circles is that of Discussion Director. You might say the following.

One of the important jobs one of you will have when we meet in our Literature Circles is to keep the discussion going. The person who does this is called the Discussion Director. It is this person's job to get your group talking about what you have read. To do this, you need to ask questions that could have more than one answer like, "What were you thinking when you read this section?" "What did you think when . . . ?" "Why do you think the author wrote this?"

7. Read the selection aloud to the group. Model the use of questions and how you use sticky notes to record your thinking as you read.

8. Discuss with students the role of Discussion Director. Explain that you will be giving them some sample questions to use to help them get started and that they should be thinking of more good questions as they read.

9. Provide a short, easy text for students to read silently. Ask them to think of one or two questions they could ask their group as they read. Ask them to write them on their sticky notes and place them in the text.

10. When they have finished reading, form small groups and have students discuss the text using the questions they have developed.

11. When groups have finished, meet as a whole class and discuss their experiences in reading.

12. Review the Literature Circles Discussion Anchor Chart. Ask if students have ideas to add.

13. Review the role of Discussion Director and invite comments and questions.

14. On succeeding days, introduce another role by using another read aloud. Proceed in explaining the role (see descriptions on pages 105–110) and modeling it through the read aloud. Follow up with discussion about that role. Provide an opportunity for students to practice the role in small groups, using short, easy text.

15. Continue until all roles have been introduced and modeled. Depending on group sizes, roles to consider including might be, *Discussion Director, *Word Wizard, Artful Artist, Literary Luminary, *Connector, and Summarizer. (Note: * Key roles)

Week 2

1. Review the Discussion Anchor Chart and the roles that have been introduced and modeled.

2. Provide a short text and explain to students that this week they will each have a different job when they meet in their small groups.

3. Distribute the role sheets (see reproducibles on pages 105–110), sticky notes, and the text.

4. Have students read the selection silently and prepare for the discussion according to the role sheet they have been given.

5. When ready, move students into small groups and have them initiate their discussions. Circulate among the groups to provide guidance and answer questions about the roles and procedures.

6. When groups have completed their discussions, reconvene as a whole group and debrief on the experience. Clarify roles and invite additional ideas for the Literature Circles Discussion Anchor Chart.

7. Begin introducing the books that students will have an opportunity to select when they begin reading and discussing longer, more complex text in their Literature Circles.

8. Review how to choose "just right" books, those that are not too hard, not too easy, but are just right for reading.

9. Do a short book talk for each book and pass the books around the room for students to peruse or make the books available in the classroom for students to review.

10. After all of the books have been introduced and students have had a chance to review them, have students list their top three preferences and submit them.

11. Form groups based on students' book preferences, appropriate reading levels, and complementary personalities.

12. Explain to students that if they don't get to read their first choice book this time, they will have an opportunity to read the book, either independently or as a member of a group, in the next Literature Circle cycle.

13. Students meet in their small groups with the text they have chosen and decide how many pages they will read before their first meeting. (The teacher helps groups chunk the text into reading segments to fit the timeframe established.) Students preview the text and discuss what they may already know about the genre, author, or topic and why they wanted to read the book.

14. Assign roles to specific students for their initial Literature Circle experience. After students begin meeting in their Literature Circles regularly, students can choose how to rotate roles among all group members or interact without specific roles.

15. The process described in the box on the next page continues until students have finished reading the text. Then new materials are selected, new groups are formed, and the discussion continues around the next text.

16. Approximately once a week, students are asked to evaluate themselves related to the Literature Circle experience (see reproducibles on pages 111–112).

Sample Schedule for Literature Circles

MONDAY	TUESDAY	WEDNESDAY	THURSDAY	FRIDAY
• Teacher presents a mini-lesson. • Students read and mark pages in text using sticky notes. • Students prepare for discussion according to their assigned roles.	• Teacher presents a mini-lesson. • Groups meet, discuss, select the next pages to read in the text, and choose roles for the next discussion. • Teacher circulates among groups, noting ideas for discussion and needs for future mini-lessons. • Students and teacher debrief.	• Teacher presents a mini-lesson. • Students read and track their thinking using sticky notes. • Students prepare for discussion according to their assigned roles.	• Teacher presents a mini-lesson. • Groups meet, discuss, select the next pages to read, and choose roles. • Students and teacher debrief.	• Teacher presents a mini-lesson. • Some groups may meet, others may use journals or other response modes to react to the text and their discussions. • Students complete self-evaluations. • Teacher may introduce new materials.

References

Daniels, H. (1994). *Literature circles: Voice and choice in the student-centered classroom.* Portland, ME: Stenhouse.

Daniels, H. (2002). *Literature circles: Voice and choice in book clubs and reading groups* (2nd ed.). Portland, ME: Stenhouse.

Fountas, I. C., & Pinnell, G. S. (2000). *Guiding readers and writers (grades 3–6): Teaching comprehension, genre, and content literacy.* Portsmouth, NH: Heinemann.

Harvey, S., & Goudvis, A. (2000). *Strategies that work: Teaching comprehension to enhance understanding.* Portland, ME: Stenhouse.

Stein, D., & Beed, P. L. (2004). Bridging the gap between fiction and nonfiction in the literature circle setting. *The Reading Teacher, 57,* 510–518.

Name _____ Date _____

Title of Our Reading _____

Literature Circle Planning Sheet

DATE	PAGES READ FOR TODAY	MY JOB TODAY	HOW WE DID TODAY	PAGES I NEED TO READ FOR THE NEXT TIME	MY JOB FOR THE NEXT TIME WE MEET

Name _____ Date _____

Group _____ Book _____

Pages _____ to _____

Discussion Director

Your job is to think about the important ideas in the reading and develop questions that your group will discuss. As you read, think about the big ideas and what interests you the most. When your group meets, begin by asking the questions you have written. Here are some sample questions to help get you started.

- What were you thinking as you read this?
- What surprised you in the reading?
- What do you think about . . . ? (put in an idea from the reading)
- Why do you think the author wrote this?
- How have you felt like one of the characters in the story?
- What do you think will happen next? What makes you think so?

Here is a place for you to write additional questions or to place your sticky notes.

_____

_____

_____

_____

_____

_____

_____

_____

_____

Jerry L. Johns, Susan Davis Lenski, and Roberta L. Berglund. *Comprehension and Vocabulary Strategies for the Elementary Grades* (2nd ed.). Copyright © 2006 by Kendall/Hunt Publishing Company (1-800-247-3458, ext. 4).

Name _____ Date _____

Group _____ Book _____

Pages _____ to _____

Artful Artist

Your job is to make a drawing of something from the reading. You might draw one or more of the following:

- the "big idea"
- an important scene
- one of the characters

- an exciting part
- the setting

Here is a place for you to do your drawing. You may also use a separate sheet of paper. When your group meets, be ready to show your drawing and tell your group:

- What the picture means
- Why you chose to draw it

- How the drawing may help to understand the story
- If there is a specific section of the text that it relates to

Name _____ Date _____

Group _____ Book _____

Pages _____ to _____

Connector

Your job is make connections between what you are reading and what you are studying or to things you know about in or outside of school. You could think about connections to:

- news events
- another book
- an experience you have had

Here is a place for you to put your sticky notes about the connections you make. Be sure to note the page numbers so that members of your group might find the ideas in the text.

📖 Word Wizard

Your job is to notice words in the reading that you think are worth knowing and remembering. These might be:

- words you like
- words you don't know
- words that are used in an interesting or unusual way
- words that help to make the story clear
- words that are used often in the text

Here is a place for you to write your words or to place your sticky notes. Be sure to note the page where each word appears.

Literary Luminary

Your job is to find parts of the text to read aloud to your group. You might choose passages that are:

- interesting
- exciting
- funny
- using interesting language

- confusing
- important to the story
- well written

Here is a place for you to place your sticky notes about the sections of text you will read aloud and why you chose it. Be sure to write down the page and paragraph numbers where the sections can be found. Be sure to practice reading each section you choose more than once so that your group members will enjoy listening to you.

Name _____ Date _____

Group _____ Book _____

Pages _____ to _____

Summarizer

Your job is to prepare a brief summary of the reading. Use these ideas to help you decide what to include.

- What was the "big idea" in this section?
- What changes did you notice in the characters?
- What might be important to remember from this section of the text?
- If you had to tell someone else about this part of the reading, what would you say?

Here is a place for you to put your sticky notes about ideas you might use in your summary. You also need to write your summary below and be ready to share it with your group.

My Summary:

_____

_____

_____

_____

Name _____ Date _____

Title _____ Pages _____

How I Did Today

Circle one rating sentence in each category.

	1	2	3	4
Reading	I did not read my assignment.	I read some of the assignment.	I read all of the assignment once.	I read the assignment more than once.
Writing • used sticky notes • wrote in my journal • did my Job Sheet	I did not do the writing.	I did some of the writing.	I did the assigned writing with some examples from the reading.	I did all of the assigned writing and used lots of ideas and examples from the reading.
Discussion • stayed on the topic when I talked • asked questions • shared my ideas from my Job Sheet	I did not talk.	I offered a few ideas.	I actively participated in the discussion.	I offered good ideas and helped to keep the discussion in my group going.
Listening	I did not listen to the other members of my group.	I listened some of the time.	I tried to listen carefully to what others had to say.	I listened carefully to what others had to say and used their ideas in my responses.
Preparation	I was not prepared for my group today.	I did some of the work to prepare for my group discussion.	I did what I was asked to do to prepare for my group discussion.	I worked hard at being ready for our group discussion.

Name _____ Date _____

Title of the Reading Selection _____

Pages _____

How I Think I Did Today

Circle one rating in each category.

I shared my ideas.	Great!	OK	I Could Do Better	Comments
I spoke clearly and softly.	Great!	OK	I Could Do Better	Comments
I answered the questions.	Great!	OK	I Could Do Better	Comments
I stayed on the topic.	Great!	OK	I Could Do Better	Comments
I disagreed without hurting others' feelings.	Great!	OK	I Could Do Better	Comments
I did not interrupt when others were talking.	Great!	OK	I Could Do Better	Comments
I gave reasons for my opinions.	Great!	OK	I Could Do Better	Comments
I listened when others were speaking.	Great!	OK	I Could Do Better	Comments
I tried to go deeper into my thinking about the reading.	Great!	OK	I Could Do Better	Comments
I asked good questions.	Great!	OK	I Could Do Better	Comments
I used my assigned job to help others understand the reading.	Great!	OK	I Could Do Better	Comments

My most important contribution to the discussion was

_____.

One thing I will try to do better next time is

_____.

Multiple Meaning Map

FOCUS		TEXT		WHEN			WHY									HOW			
Comprehension	Vocabulary	Narrative	Informational	Before Reading	During Reading	After Reading	Predicting	Connecting	Questioning	Using Text Structure	Visualizing	Inferring	Summarizing	Synthesizing	Determining Importance	Individual	Partner	Small Group	Whole Group
•	•	•	•	•		•	•	•								•	•	•	•

DESCRIPTION

A Multiple Meaning Map is designed to help students remember several different meanings for a single vocabulary word. Many vocabulary strategies focus on one meaning of a word, but the Multiple Meaning Map provides a strategy for teachers to teach students to explore a variety of meanings for a word. Teachers should use the Multiple Meaning Map strategy when they want to teach more than one meaning for a word.

Teaching Goals

1. To help students expand their vocabularies.
2. To help students identify and learn multiple meanings for vocabulary words.
3. To provide a graphic for students to use to remember multiple meanings of words.

Procedure

1. Identify a word that has more than one meaning that you want students to learn. Think of as many meanings as you can before you begin the lesson. Use a dictionary, glossary, or thesaurus if necessary.
2. Make an overhead transparency of one of the Multiple Meaning Maps on pages 116–117. Choose the one that will be easiest for students to use.
3. Write the word that you want to teach in the rectangle in the center of the page. One word with multiple meanings, for example, is *tick*. If you were teaching the word *tick,* you would write it in the rectangle.

4. Ask students to think of the ways the word *tick* could be used. Discuss some of the meanings that students volunteer. Include slang definitions as well as traditional definitions. Write these definitions in the circles off the central word. Some of the meanings of *tick* follow:

   - A bloodsucking insect
   - The beat of the clock
   - A checkmark
   - To anger

5. If you have students who speak a language other than English, include a translation of the main word in the circles. Point out to the students that the word *tick* might have multiple meanings in English but not in other languages.

6. Divide the class into groups of three or four students. Have students develop a list of sentences using the word *tick* in a variety of ways. Allow students to add endings to the word. Some examples of sentences using the various meanings of *tick* follow.

   - I found 6 *ticks* in the cuff of my jeans.
   - The clock was *ticking* so loudly that I couldn't sleep.
   - Jon heard a bomb *ticking*.
   - Alison *ticked* off the list of things to do.
   - Mark *ticks* me off when he pretends he doesn't know math.

7. Have students read their sentences. If students use a word incorrectly, suggest revisions of the sentences so that the word fits the sentence. If students have difficulty writing sentences for some of the meanings, provide sample sentences for them.

8. After students understand how to use the Multiple Meaning Map, have them use dictionaries, glossaries, and thesauruses to find multiple meanings of words independently.

9. Two versions of Multiple Meaning Maps are on pages 116–117. Use the one that best fits your situation.

Multiple Meaning Map

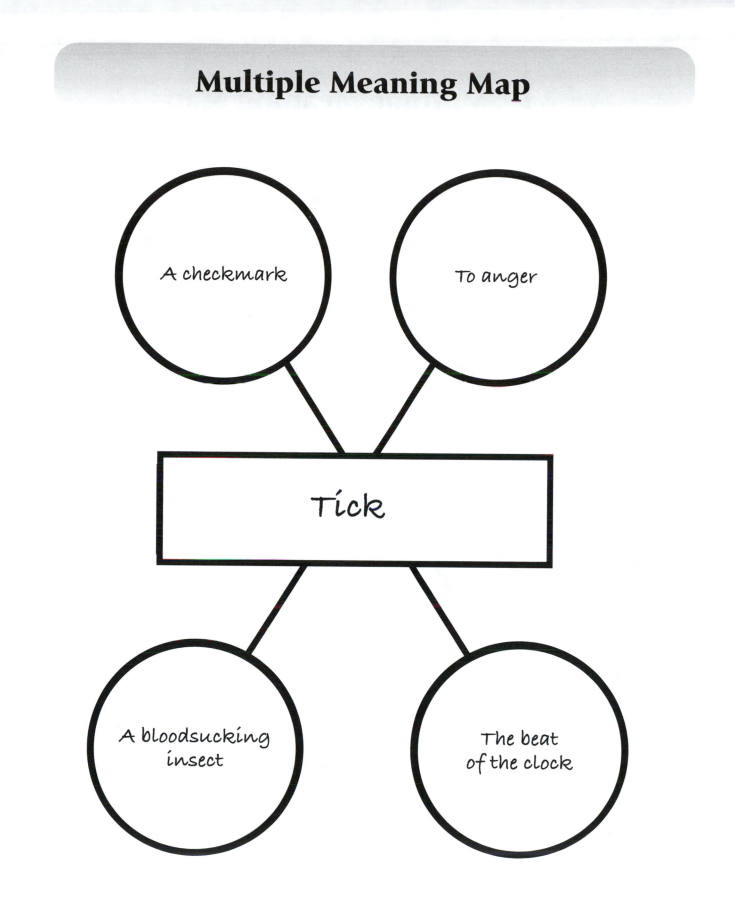

A checkmark

To anger

Tick

A bloodsucking insect

The beat of the clock

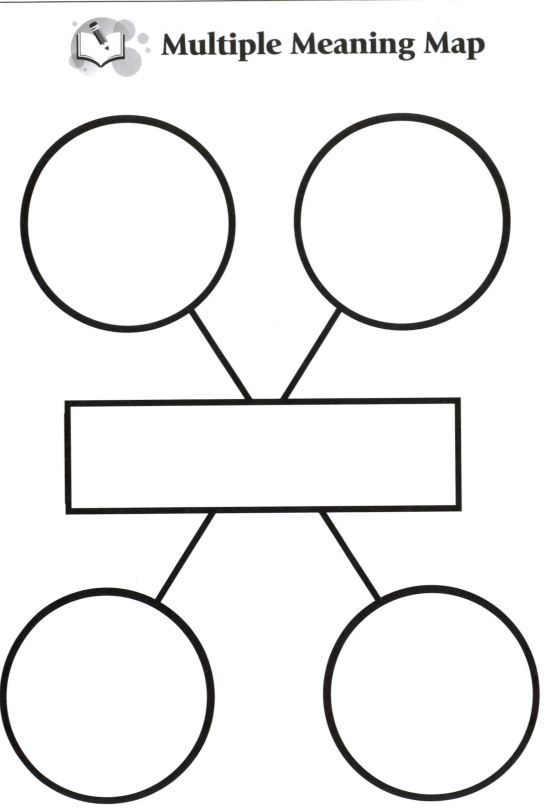

Multiple Meaning Map

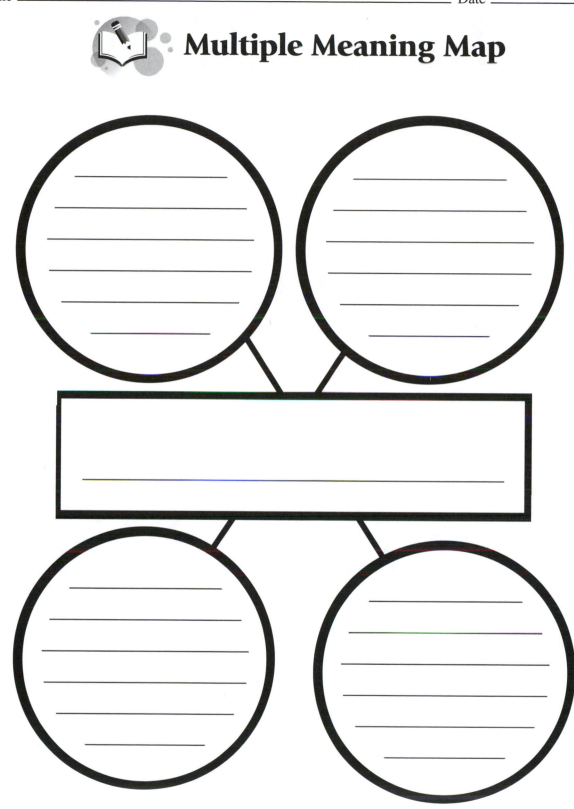

Multiple Meaning Map

Mystery Word Bubbles

FOCUS		TEXT		WHEN			WHY									HOW			
Comprehension	Vocabulary	Narrative	Informational	Before Reading	During Reading	After Reading	Predicting	Connecting	Questioning	Using Text Structure	Visualizing	Inferring	Summarizing	Synthesizing	Determining Importance	Individual	Partner	Small Group	Whole Group
	•		•			•		•						•		•			

DESCRIPTION

Mystery Word Bubbles (Richardson & Morgan, 2006) are similar to Semantic Maps (see page 187) and Concept Circles (see page 33) and can be used as a scaffolding experience to lead students into these related strategies. Mystery Word Bubbles should be used as a postreading activity for review and to reinforce key concepts from a unit of study.

Teaching Goals

1. To help students connect vocabulary to a concept or main idea.
2. To invite students to classify words that are related to various concepts and ideas.
3. To provide a means for students to review and reinforce key concepts and vocabulary from a reading selection or unit of study.

Procedure

1. Select the key concept words that you wish students to know. Draw an oval shape with three lines drawn vertically from the oval for each concept word or use the reproducible master on page 123. You may also wish to make an overhead transparency of How to Solve Mystery Word Bubbles on page 122.

2. Place one clue word or phrase related to each key concept word on one of the three legs extending downward from its oval. For younger or less able students, you may wish to place word or phrase clues on more than one of the legs.

3. Provide students with a list of vocabulary words, including the key concept words, selected from the unit of study. For example, in studying the solar system, choose words that name some of the planets, as well as characteristics unique to the individual planets. Refer to the example on page 121.

4. Invite students to use the clue words or phrases from the legs below the ovals to solve the mystery concept word that should go in each oval. You might say the following.

> We have been studying our solar system. To help us review what we have learned, I have created some mysteries for you to solve. I have given you some clues, and now you need to be good detectives. Remember to think about what you know about the planets in our solar system and see if you can use my clues and your good detective skills to figure out the mystery words.

> Let's do one together. The first Mystery Word Bubble has the word *largest* written as a clue below it. Does anyone remember what the largest planet is? [Elicit the correct response, *Jupiter.*]

> You have solved the first part of the mystery by correctly identifying Jupiter as the largest planet in our solar system. Now let's solve the rest of the mystery by figuring out which of the remaining clues will tell us more about Jupiter. [Continue working with students until they have added *made of gas* and *red spot.*]

5. Students should use additional clues and phrases to help them solve the remaining Mystery Word Bubbles.

6. As students become more proficient with this strategy, you may wish to eliminate the use of a word list and have students use their textbooks and other reference sources to solve the word mysteries. You may also wish to provide them with copies of the reproducible master How to Solve Mystery Word Bubbles on page 122.

7. Students enjoy making Mystery Word Bubbles for others to solve. Their work can be reproduced and placed in one of the classroom's learning centers for use in independent or small group work.

Reference

Richardson, J. S., & Morgan, R. F. (2006). *Reading to learn in the content areas* (6th ed.). Belmont, CA: Wadsworth.

Mystery Word Bubbles

⇒ **DIRECTIONS**
Solve the following word mysteries.

Planets
_____
Topic

Word Clues

- largest planet
- Earth
- has water
- red spot

- second planet from sun
- oxygen
- Mercury
- closest to the sun

- hottest planet
- Jupiter
- Earth's twin
- living things

- made of gas
- Venus
- smallest
- bright

Mystery Word Bubbles

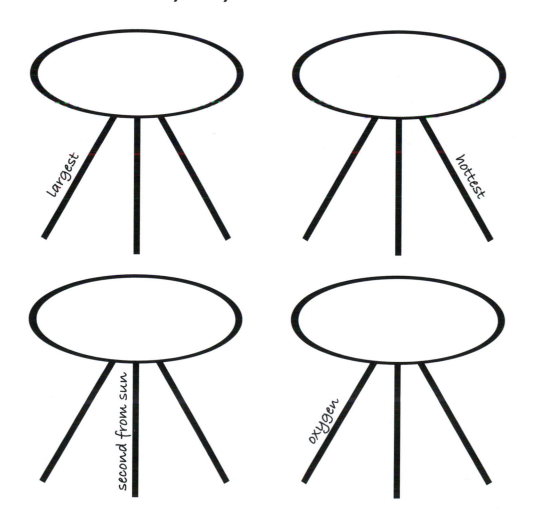

How to Solve Mystery Word Bubbles

Can you be a word detective and use the clues to solve the word mysteries?

1. Look at the word or phrase on the line below one of the bubbles.

2. Now look at the list of words. What big idea does the clue word below the bubble make you think of?

3. When you think you know the bubble word, write that word inside the bubble.

4. Now look at the word list again. Are there other words that go with the one you have written inside the bubble?

5. Write those words on the lines below the bubble. You have solved one of the mysteries!

6. Now see if you can solve the remaining word mysteries.

Mystery Word Bubbles

➤ **DIRECTIONS**

Solve the following word mysteries.

_____
Topic

Word Clues

_____   _____   _____

_____   _____   _____

_____   _____   _____

_____   _____   _____

Mystery Word Bubbles

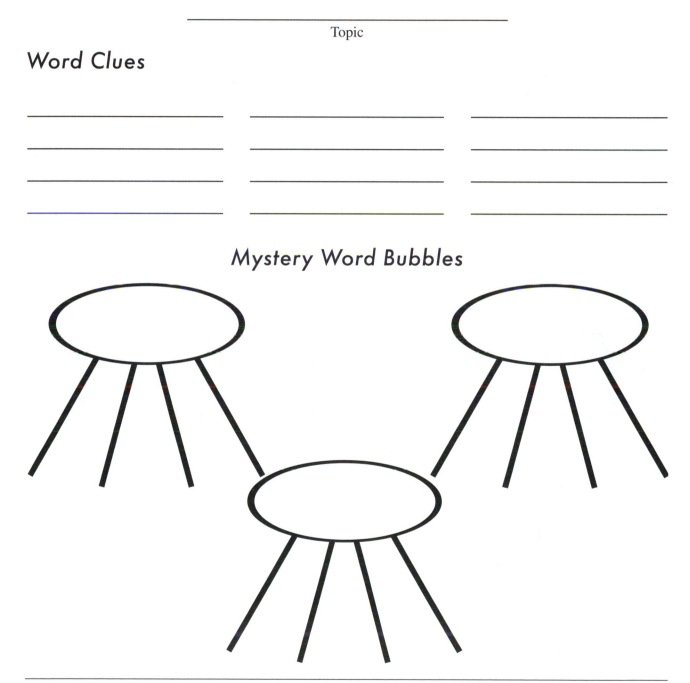

Name _____ Date _____

Mystery Word Bubbles

➥ **DIRECTIONS**

Solve the following word mysteries.

_____

Topic

Word Clues

_____   _____   _____

_____   _____   _____

_____   _____   _____

Mystery Word Bubbles

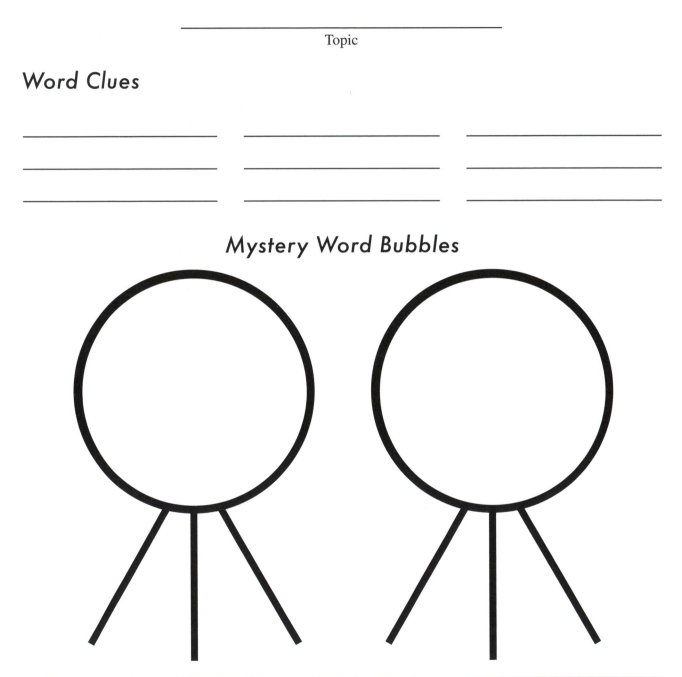

Name _____ Date _____

Mystery Word Bubbles

⇒ **DIRECTIONS**
Solve the following word mysteries.

_____
Topic

Word Clues

_____   _____   _____

_____   _____   _____

_____   _____   _____

_____   _____   _____

_____   _____   _____

_____   _____   _____

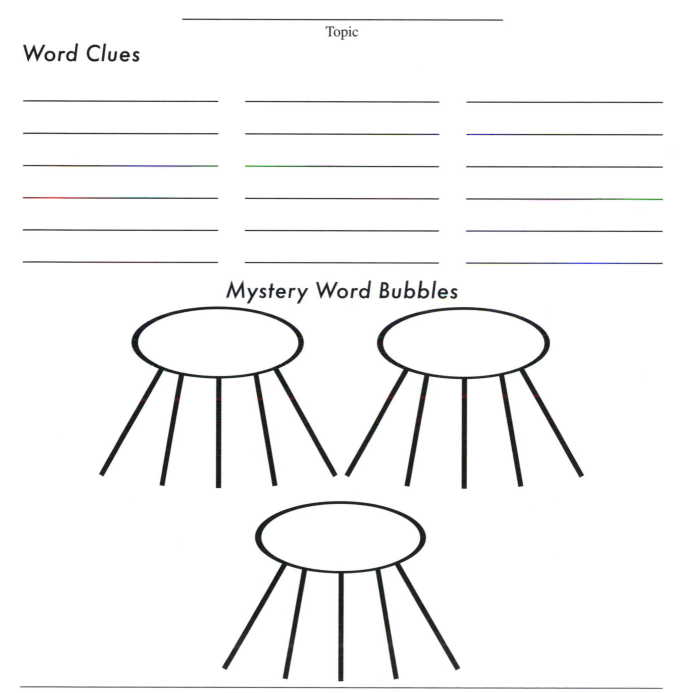

Mystery Word Bubbles

Paired Questioning

FOCUS		TEXT		WHEN			WHY									HOW			
Comprehension	Vocabulary	Narrative	Informational	Before Reading	During Reading	After Reading	Predicting	Connecting	Questioning	Using Text Structure	Visualizing	Inferring	Summarizing	Synthesizing	Determining Importance	Individual	Partner	Small Group	Whole Group
•		•	•		•	•	•	•	•			•					•		

DESCRIPTION

Paired Questioning (McLaughlin & Allen, 2002; Vaughan & Estes, 1986) involves putting students in pairs, having them read short segments of narrative or informational text, and then questioning each other about its content. Paired Questioning is an adaptation of the ReQuest procedure developed by Manzo (1969). Paired Questioning gives students practice in developing questions on a variety of levels and helps students learn to select and defend their choices regarding the main ideas and important details in a text.

Teaching Goals

1. To actively engage students in a reading selection.
2. To provide an opportunity for students to ask and answer questions while reading a selection.
3. To encourage students to ask a variety of questions.
4. To help students understand a reading selection.

Procedure

1. Divide the class into pairs of students.
2. Share the guidelines of the Paired Questioning procedure (see page 129) with students and explain it as needed.

3. When students understand the guidelines, invite students to begin by reading the title or chapter heading of the text. You might model the procedure by reading aloud to the class the title from the book, *How Animals Move* (Byrne, 1998).

4. Next, put the book aside and invite students to ask you a question about the book. You might hold up the book and say the following.

> Mrs. Shafer: I just read the title of this book aloud to you. Can one of you ask me a question about the book?
>
> Jasper: What do you think this book will be about?
>
> Mrs. Shafer: I think this book might help me learn more about how different kinds of animals move. I did the best I could to answer your question. Now, without showing you the book again, I am going to ask you a question about the book. Why is movement important to an animal's survival?

This is an important opportunity to model a question involving an inference or one that engenders higher-level thinking.

5. After a student has answered your question, repeat the modeling with a short segment of text or the contents page, if appropriate.

6. Continue to model the Paired Questioning procedure until you believe that students understand it. Then refer students again to the Paired Questioning procedure (see page 129) and have them continue reading and posing questions with their partners.

7. In order to continue modeling good questioning techniques, you may wish to use the strategy when reading aloud to students in small and large group settings.

8. As an alternative to Paired Questioning, you may want to have students use the Say Something strategy (Short, Harste, & Burke, 1996) at the stopping points in the text instead of asking and answering questions.

References

Byrne, D. (1998). *How animals move.* Barrington, IL: Rigby.

Manzo, A. V. (1969). ReQuest procedure. *Journal of Reading, 13,* 123–126.

McLaughlin, M., & Allen, M. B. (2002). *Guided comprehension: A teaching model for grades 3–8.* Newark, DE: International Reading Association.

Short, K. G., Harste, J. C., & Burke, C. (1996). *Creating classrooms for authors and inquirers.* Portsmouth, NH: Heinemann.

Vaughan, J. L., & Estes, T. H. (1986). *Reading and reasoning beyond the primary grades.* Boston: Allyn and Bacon.

Paired Questioning

Getting Started

1. Find a quiet place.
2. Be sure you can see the words and illustrations clearly.
3. Read the title or heading to yourself.
4. Close the book or turn it over.
5. Ask your partner a question and listen to the answer.
6. Have your partner ask you a question. Answer it.
7. Be sure you and your partner agree on the answers to the questions. Reread to see if you are correct.

Keep Going

1. Read some more of the book to yourself. Think of another question to ask your partner.
2. Close the book again (or turn it over). Ask your partner your question and then try to answer your partner's question.

When You Are Finished Reading

1. Think of the most important ideas from your reading.
2. Tell your partner your ideas. Does your partner agree with you? What are your partner's ideas?
3. If you have time, draw a picture of the most important ideas from your reading and write a short summary of your reading to share with the rest of the class.

Jerry L. Johns, Susan Davis Lenski, and Roberta L. Berglund. *Comprehension and Vocabulary Strategies for the Elementary Grades* (2nd ed.). Copyright © 2006 by Kendall/Hunt Publishing Company (1-800-247-3458, ext. 4). May be reproduced for noncommercial educational purposes within the guidelines noted on the copyright page.

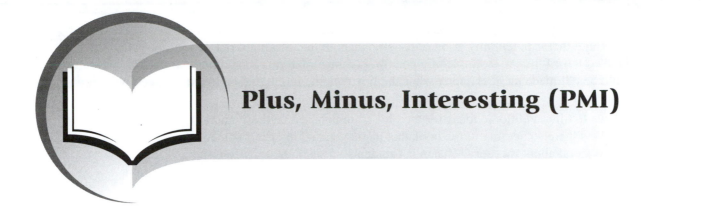

Plus, Minus, Interesting (PMI)

FOCUS		TEXT		WHEN			WHY									HOW			
Comprehension	Vocabulary	Narrative	Informational	Before Reading	During Reading	After Reading	Predicting	Connecting	Questioning	Using Text Structure	Visualizing	Inferring	Summarizing	Synthesizing	Determining Importance	Individual	Partner	Small Group	Whole Group
•		•	•			•		•				•				•	•	•	•

DESCRIPTION

Plus, Minus, Interesting (PMI), (deBono, 1992), involves students in constructing meaning from and responding to a text after reading. This reflective activity invites students to analyze text for its positive, negative, and interesting features, as well as for information and/or impact. PMI encourages students to make connections with and formulate opinions about material they have listened to or read.

Teaching Goals

1. To actively engage students while reading.
2. To provide a means for students to react to a reading selection.
3. To have students make judgments about the content of a reading selection.

Procedure

1. Make a transparency using the reproducible master on page 134 or draw a PMI organizer on the board. Create columns for P (Plus), M (Minus), and I (Interesting).
2. Read a portion of a text (either narrative or informational) aloud to students. For example, a story that could be read aloud to primary students might be *The Velveteen Rabbit* (Williams, 1958).

3. Following the reading, record something you liked about the text. In the case of informational text, record something that is potentially good or beneficial about the information. Put your ideas under the column labeled P for Plus. An example of a positive comment that might be written about *The Velveteen Rabbit* could be, "It made me feel happy when the boy took the rabbit that he loved so much with him wherever he went."

4. Invite students to offer additional ideas for the Plus column based on their reactions to the text. You might ask, "Was there something in the book that made you feel happy or something that you thought was especially good about the story?" Then list students' ideas in the Plus column.

5. Now move to the Minus (M) column. Here you should list something you did not like about the text. In the case of informational text, list some bad or negative impact the information discussed may have had. For example, a minus for *The Velveteen Rabbit* might be, "I felt sorry for the Velveteen Rabbit when the real rabbits made fun of him. Teasing hurts." Once you have offered an idea or two, invite students to suggest additional thoughts for the M column and record them.

6. The final column is the Interesting (I) column. Now it is your turn to record something interesting about what was read. For example, you might say, "To me it was interesting that children sometimes think their special toys are real." Students then have a turn to add the ideas that they found interesting to the I column on the chart.

7. After this strategy has been modeled with one type of text, provide copies of the reproducible master on page 134 for students to use as they read a text of the same genre independently or with a partner.

8. When students have completed the reading and their PMI sheets, they should use them in a small or large group discussion. Students then have an opportunity to share their ideas with others and listen to the comments generated by other group members.

References

deBono, E. (1992). *Serious creativity.* New York: Harper.

Williams, M. (1958). *The velveteen rabbit.* New York: Doubleday.

The Velveteen Rabbit

Title

PLUS +	MINUS −	INTERESTING
It made me feel happy when the boy took the rabbit that he loved so much with him wherever he went.	I felt sorry for the velveteen Rabbit when the real rabbits made fun of him. Teasing hurts.	It was interesting that children sometimes think their special toys are real.

Jerry L. Johns, Susan Davis Lenski, and Roberta L. Berglund. *Comprehension and Vocabulary Strategies for the Elementary Grades* (2nd ed.). Copyright © 2006 by Kendall/Hunt Publishing Company (1-800-247-3458, ext. 4). May be reproduced for noncommercial educational purposes within the guidelines noted on the copyright page.

Name _____ Date _____

Title

PLUS +	MINUS –	INTERESTING

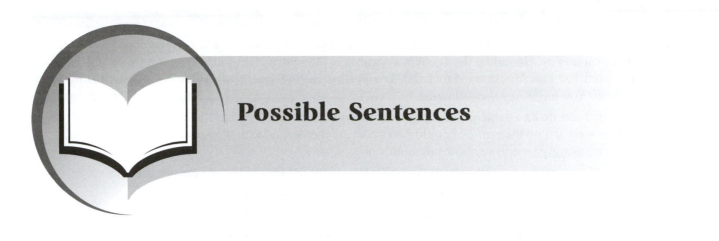

Possible Sentences

FOCUS		TEXT		WHEN			WHY									HOW			
Comprehension	Vocabulary	Narrative	Informational	Before Reading	During Reading	After Reading	Predicting	Connecting	Questioning	Using Text Structure	Visualizing	Inferring	Summarizing	Synthesizing	Determining Importance	Individual	Partner	Small Group	Whole Group
•	•		•	•	•	•	•	•				•				•	•		•

DESCRIPTION

Possible Sentences (Moore & Moore, 2004) is a strategy that will help students predict the content of a selection. They then check their predictions while reading or listening. After reading, students use the text to support the accuracy of their sentences or revise them so they become more reflective of the content. The Possible Sentences strategy helps students set a purpose for reading or listening and develops an interest in and curiosity about the text.

Teaching Goals

1. To have students predict how vocabulary might be used in a reading selection.
2. To invite students to connect vocabulary words in a meaningful way.
3. To have students evaluate their predictions after reading a selection.

Procedure

1. Identify 6 to 10 key vocabulary words (some new, some familiar) from a selected text. Write them on the board, overhead transparency, or reproducible master (page 137 or 138) and pronounce the words for the students.

2. Model the strategy using two of the words in a single sentence. Write the sentence on the board or overhead transparency. Underline the vocabulary words in the sentence. For example, the following words are from *You Can Measure* (Mansk, 2003): *ruler, measuring tape, scale, plant, kitten, measuring cup,* and *food.* You might say the following.

> Let's see if I can make a sentence using the words *scale* and *kitten.* Perhaps the book will say, "The *kitten* was weighed on the *scale.*" I could also make another sentence with *measuring tape* and *plant.* "I used a <u>measuring tape</u> to see how tall mom's <u>plant</u> was."

3. Continue writing sentences together with the students until all the vocabulary words are used.

4. Direct students to read the text selection or read it together as a class.

5. After reading the selection, reread each Possible Sentence with students to determine its accuracy. For beginning readers, you may want to use a *star* for true, a *sad face* for an inaccurate prediction, and a *question mark* for those you aren't sure of because adequate information is not available. For students in grades two and above, a *T* can be used for true, an *F* for false, and *DK* for don't know. Encourage students to cite specific text references to support their conclusions about the accuracy of the sentences.

6. You may choose to correct the statements that are inaccurate. Students in grades two and above could do research for further information or the don't know statements.

7. When the activity is repeated, students (if they are writing), can do the activity using the reproducible master on page 137 or page 138.

References

Mansk, A. (2003). *You can measure.* New York: Sadlier-Oxford.

Moore, D. W., Moore, S. A. (1992). Possible sentences. In J. E. Readence, T. W. Bean, & R. S. Baldwin (Eds.), *Content area literacy* (8th ed.) (pp. 220–221). Dubuque, IA: Kendall/Hunt.

Name _____ Date _____

Possible Sentences

_____
Title of Selection

Below are some words you will find in your reading.

_____   _____

_____   _____

_____   _____

_____   _____

_____   _____

Possible Sentences

➥ **DIRECTIONS**

Write one or more sentences using at least two of the above words in each sentence. Underline the words you use from the list above. After reading, rate the sentences by using the following key:

⭐ = **true**   ☹ = **false**   ❓ = **don't know**

_____ 1. _____

        _____

_____ 2. _____

        _____

_____ 3. _____

        _____

_____ 4. _____

        _____

Name _____ Date _____

 **Possible Sentences**

_____
Title of Selection

Below are some words you will find in your reading.

_____   _____

_____   _____

_____   _____

_____   _____

_____   _____

Possible Sentences

➥ **DIRECTIONS**

Write one or more sentences using at least two of the above words in each sentence. Underline the words you use from the list above. After reading, rate the sentences by using the following key:

           T = true   F = false   DK = don't know

_____ 1. _____

            _____

_____ 2. _____

            _____

_____ 3. _____

            _____

_____ 4. _____

            _____

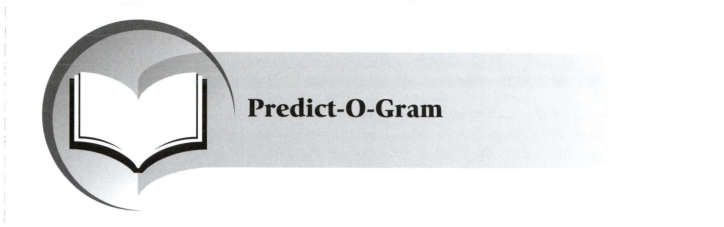

Predict-O-Gram

FOCUS		TEXT		WHEN			WHY									HOW			
Comprehension	Vocabulary	Narrative	Informational	Before Reading	During Reading	After Reading	Predicting	Connecting	Questioning	Using Text Structure	Visualizing	Inferring	Summarizing	Synthesizing	Determining Importance	Individual	Partner	Small Group	Whole Group
•	•	•		•	•	•	•		•	•		•				•	•	•	•

DESCRIPTION

A Predict-O-Gram (Blachowicz, 1986) invites students to use their knowledge of story structure to assign words to categories prior to reading. Examples of the categories include setting, characters, and actions. The teacher selects the words to be categorized. Students can discuss reasons for their placement of words prior to reading. After reading, students can compare their predictions with the text and revise the Predict-O-Gram.

Teaching Goals

1. To encourage students to use story structure to classify vocabulary words prior to reading.
2. To provide an opportunity for students to predict what a story might be about.
3. To have students evaluate the accuracy of their predictions within the context of story structure.
4. To encourage students to actively discuss story content to help promote comprehension and understanding.

Procedure

1. Use items 1–3 if students do not understand basic story structure, and take time to help them acquire such knowledge. You might begin by telling a story and clearly stating the story elements and writing them on the board. Create your own story or use the example below.

    Erica and Emily decided to practice kicking a soccer ball. They looked and looked all over the house, but they couldn't find the ball. They decided to ask their dad. Dad suggested that they look in the hall closet. Sure enough! The ball was tucked in the corner of the closet under a jacket that had fallen on it. The girls took the ball to the back yard and began to practice by kicking the ball.

2. Guide students to understand the basic story elements. You might say the following.

    There are ways that all stories are alike. Stories have characters; they can be people or animals. Who are the characters in this story? Tell me and I'll write them under *characters*. [As students share, write the names of the characters.] Guide students as needed (e.g., Who else is mentioned in the story?) and address or clarify incorrect responses.

    Stories also have a setting—that means they take place somewhere at some time. Where does this story take place? [Have students share and write words under the category *setting* or *place*.]

    A story also has a problem or conflict. Who can tell me the problem? I'll write it under *problem*. [Clarify as needed.] Finally, stories have a solution. Solution means how the problem is solved. What is the solution in our story? I'll write it on the board.

3. Highlight the basic story elements from your example and help students understand that all stories have these basic elements. Take time to develop an understanding of story structure using additional examples and/or by reading stories to the class. You may develop this understanding through multiple exposures to stories and through intentionally focused instruction. Consider using some of the following ideas.

    *   Oral stories that use your students' names and familiar locations
    *   Nursery rhymes
    *   Common stories such as *The Three Little Pigs*
    *   *Aunt Isabel Tells a Good One* (Duke, 1992)—an excellent, engaging introduction to story grammar for students

4. When you believe students possess a basic knowledge of story structure, introduce the Predict-O-Gram to the entire class or to a small group of students. Adapt the Predict-O-Gram to suit your students' needs. Help students connect their knowledge of story structure to the Predict-O-Gram by saying something like the following.

    As we've shared stories orally and through reading, you have learned that all stories have settings, characters, problems, and solutions. [Review as necessary.] Today we'll use our knowledge of stories to predict where certain words from the story might fit on this chart. [Highlight chart elements as needed.]

5. From a simple story that is unfamiliar to students, select several key words. List the words on the board, chart paper, overhead transparency, or on a reproduced copy of a Predict-O-Gram (pages 142–143).

6. Use whole group or small group instruction the first time you introduce the Predict-O-Gram. You can gradually move to more independent work as students exhibit readiness and understanding.

7. Invite students to predict what will happen in the story by suggesting words from the list in the boxes of the Predict-O-Gram. As students share their predictions, write them in the chart. If necessary, read the words to the students. Encourage students to give reasons for their choices.

8. When all the words have been placed in the Predict-O-Gram, invite students to predict what the story might be about. The particular words you choose for the strategy can help determine the degree of difficulty. Then read the story to students or, if appropriate, have students read it independently.

9. After the story has been read, use the Predict-O-Gram to review the predictions as compared to the story. Words may be moved to the correct places on the Predict-O-Gram. Some teachers use a magnetic white board and word cards to make it easier to move words. Other teachers use chart paper and word cards with tape on the back so words can be moved.

10. Help students understand that this strategy can help them think about the parts or elements in all stories they read or hear. This knowledge of the elements will help them remember the story.

Predict-O-Gram

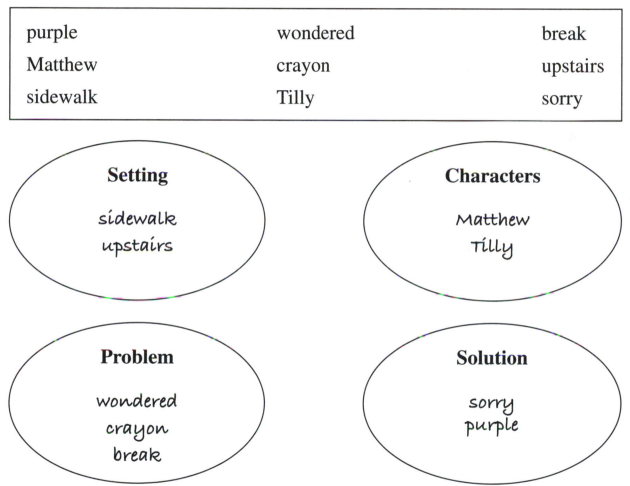

purple	wondered	break
Matthew	crayon	upstairs
sidewalk	Tilly	sorry

Setting
sidewalk
upstairs

Characters
Matthew
Tilly

Problem
wondered
crayon
break

Solution
sorry
purple

11. Two Predict-O-Gram reproducible masters can be found on pages 142–143. One is intended for early experiences with this strategy; the other can be used with older students and to expand the basic elements of a story. The Predict-O-Gram can also be used to help students structure their writing. Words for their stories can be placed in the Predict-O-Gram and then crossed out or checked off as they are used in the story.

References

Blachowicz, C. L. Z. (1986). Making connections: Alternatives to the vocabulary notebook. *Journal of Reading, 29,* 643–649.

Duke, K. (1992). *Aunt Isabel tells a good one.* New York: Puffin.

Name _____ Date _____

Predict-O-Gram

➤ **DIRECTIONS**
Put the words where you think they fit best. Write them on the lines in the boxes.

_____   _____   _____

_____   _____   _____

_____   _____   _____

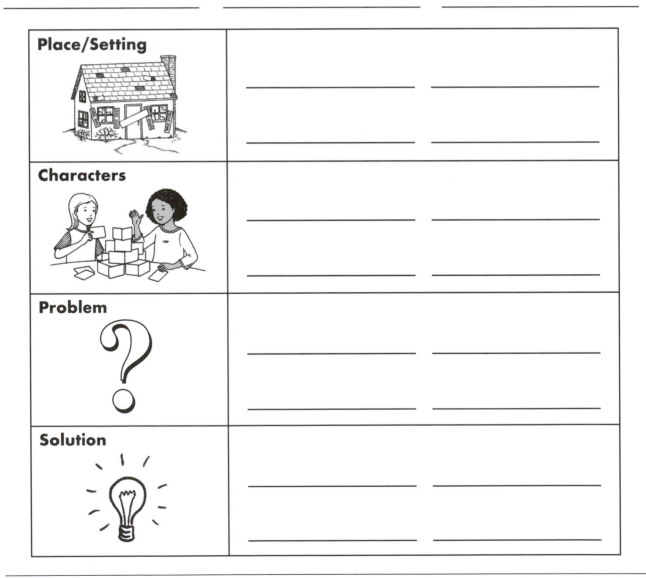

Name _____ Date _____

Predict-O-Gram

_____
Title

⇒ DIRECTIONS

How do you think these words will be used in the story? Write them in a square on the Predict-O-Gram. You may have more than one word in a square.

_____

_____

_____

_____

Setting	Characters	Goal or Problem
Events or Something That Happens	**Solution**	**Other Things**

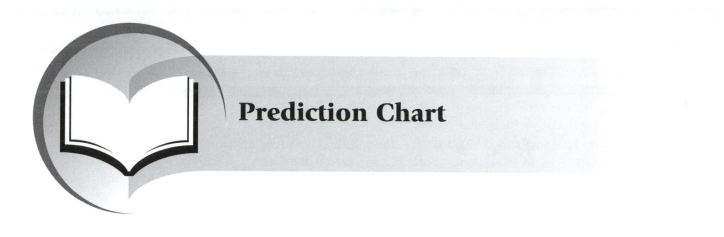

Prediction Chart

FOCUS		TEXT		WHEN			WHY									HOW			
Comprehension	Vocabulary	Narrative	Informational	Before Reading	During Reading	After Reading	Predicting	Connecting	Questioning	Using Text Structure	Visualizing	Inferring	Summarizing	Synthesizing	Determining Importance	Individual	Partner	Small Group	Whole Group
•		•	•	•	•		•		•							•	•	•	•

DESCRIPTION

A Prediction Chart is an organizational tool for students to use as they make and confirm predictions before and during reading. Before reading, students should make predictions based on the title, front cover, and illustrations of the story. As students read, they should continue to make and confirm or revise their predictions to deepen their comprehension of the story. Teachers can use Prediction Charts during Shared Reading, and they can also encourage students to use them while reading independently. Most students will need to have the Prediction Chart demonstrated several times with different selections.

Teaching Goals

1. To engage students in making predictions prior to reading and to evaluate those predictions during reading.
2. To have students use text features as a basis for making predictions.
3. To encourage students to make predictions when reading independently.

Procedure

1. Tell students that they should think about the title of a story before they begin reading. Explain that when they think about the story before reading, they are getting their minds ready to read. You might use a computer analogy with some students similar to the example below.

   I'm going to read a new book titled *Wolf!* (Bloom, 1999). When I read the title, I boot up the "computer files" in my mind on the things I know about wolves. In my mind, I have all sorts of information about wolves, stories about wolves, and the time I saw a wolf in Alaska. All of this information is in my mind, much like a folder in a computer titled *wolves*. I open that folder and think about all of the things I know about wolves before I begin reading the story. Some of these ideas may be helpful as I read.

2. Remind students that as they think about the title of a story, they should also look at the picture on the cover. The picture often clues readers into the kind of story it will be. For example, you might say something like the following.

   As I look at the cover of the book *Wolf!*, I notice several things. First, I notice that the title ends with an exclamation point. I've never seen a title with that type of punctuation, and I'm not sure what it means, but I think it will be a different type of wolf story. Then I look at the picture on the cover, and I find that the picture is not realistic—the animals are drawn like cartoon characters. The wolf has on a pair of glasses, and he's reading a book with a pig and a cow. A duck is looking over his shoulder.

   The picture on the cover tells me a number of things. First, I don't think the story will be real but will be made up. Second, it looks like it will be a funny story. It also will probably be something about reading because there are books on the cover and a wolf is reading.

3. Have students practice predicting by using the title and cover picture from several other books. Remind students that predicting before reading is an important part of understanding what they read.

4. At another session, draw a Prediction Chart on the board or on chart paper, or, if you have students who can read and write independently, copy one of the reproducible Prediction Charts from pages 149–151 and distribute it to students.

5. Remind students that they already learned that they should make predictions by using the title and picture on the cover for clues. Then tell students that they should also make predictions while they are reading.

6. Demonstrate the use of predictions while reading, as in the following example.

   After I read the first two pages of *Wolf!*, I stopped reading and thought about what had happened. At the beginning of the story, a hungry wolf stopped at a farm to look at the animals. The animals were reading.

   After I read these two pages, I predicted that the wolf would charge into the barnyard and grab the duck. I thought this because in many fairy tales the wolf tries to eat small animals.

7. Tell students that they can record their predictions on a Prediction Chart so that they remember what they thought. Point out the first predictions in the second column of the sample Prediction Chart under the heading, "What I am thinking about. . . ." Encourage students to make multiple predictions in this column.

8. Read several more pages of the book or have students read independently. Stop after a few pages and ask students to respond to the prompt, "Was I right? Why or why not?" Explain that many predictions are partially right and that, as they read, students should "confirm" their predictions by determining how close they were to the actual story. Show students the third column on the Prediction Chart that details how "right" the predictions were. Encourage students to use their knowledge of the story in their responses.

9. Use the Prediction Chart often, especially during read alouds, Shared Reading, guided reading, and independent reading. Model your own predictions and also elicit students' predictions. Encourage students to use a Prediction Chart as they read in pairs or independently.

10. Reproducible masters of Prediction Charts can be found on pages 149–151.

Reference

Bloom, B. (1999). *Wolf!* New York: Orchard Books.

Prediction Chart

for   *Wolf! by B. Bloom*

PART OF BOOK	WHAT I AM THINKING ABOUT . . .	WAS I RIGHT? WHY OR WHY NOT?
First two pages	The wolf would charge the animals and grab the duck.	The wolf did run out and try to scare the animals, but he didn't grab the duck.
	The wolf would ask the animals for food.	The wolf didn't ask the animals for food, but he howled.
	The wolf would eat the animals' supper.	The wolf seemed to forget he was hungry because he was so surprised that the animals weren't scared.

Name _____ Date _____

 **Prediction Chart**

for _____

PART OF BOOK	WHAT I AM THINKING ABOUT . . .	WAS I RIGHT? WHY OR WHY NOT?

Name _____ Date _____

Book Title _____

Prediction Chart

	MY PREDICTIONS	WHAT REALLY HAPPENED
Title/cover _____		
Pages _____		
Pages _____		

Name _____ Date _____

Title _____

Prediction Chart

PAGE NUMBERS	PREDICTION	CHECK (✓) IF CONFIRMED	REVISED PREDICTION

Putting Clues Together

FOCUS		TEXT		WHEN			WHY									HOW			
Comprehension	Vocabulary	Narrative	Informational	Before Reading	During Reading	After Reading	Predicting	Connecting	Questioning	Using Text Structure	Visualizing	Inferring	Summarizing	Synthesizing	Determining Importance	Individual	Partner	Small Group	Whole Group
•		•	•	•	•		•				•	•			•	•			

DESCRIPTION

Putting Clues Together (Zeigler & Johns, 2005) is a visualization strategy to help students predict, draw conclusions, make inferences, and evaluate text. Students can use the title and imagine pictures to go with it. They can also use the words in the text to create pictures and images. The goal of the strategy is to help students engage in an often neglected way to help construct meaning. In a review of the literature, Gambrell and Koskinen (2002) concluded that visualization (making mental pictures) can help students enhance both reading and listening comprehension.

Teaching Goals

1. To help students use visualization to strengthen their comprehension.
2. To assist students in achieving higher levels of comprehension.
3. To actively engage students during reading.

Procedure

1. Take time to help students realize that they use visualization to remember images or experiences in their lives and that mental pictures or images can also be used in reading. The ideas that follow have been adapted from lessons prepared by Zeigler and Johns (2005).

   - Have students picture their rooms and describe them. Invite students to sketch what they have pictured. Repeat the process with a letter of the alphabet and have students picture something that begins with that letter. Help students see that there are a variety of possible responses through sharing in small groups.

   - Collect common objects and develop descriptions or clues for each. Share the clues one at a time and invite students to guess the object. Have students raise one hand if they think they know. Students should raise both hands if they are sure they know (but they should not say anything). Two examples are provided below.

   Example 1
   My color is yellow.
   I'm about six inches long.
   I am sharp on one end.
   I have an eraser on the other end.
   (pencil)

   Example 2
   I have lots of marks on me.
   My color is tan.
   I'm used in math.
   I'm used to measure things.
   (ruler)

2. After students realize what visualization is, help them transfer the strategy to reading. Choose a book that offers clues to help students predict and infer. A wide range of students will enjoy *I Spy With My Little Eye* (Gardner, 2001) which uses details about different kinds of animals beginning with each letter of the alphabet. Students use the clues to predict, infer, draw conclusions, and/or evaluate as they put the clues together to figure out the answers.

3. Tell students that words in a book can help them create mental images or pictures. Use several examples from *I Spy With My Little Eye*. Read a clue and then invite students to make predictions supported with their reasoning. You may want to begin by using a think aloud with the example shown below.

Book Clue	*Think Aloud*
It hides in the water.	I'm picturing a goldfish or it might be a sea horse. It could also be a plant because some plants live in the water. I don't think it would be a plant; they really don't hide in the water.
It has very sharp teeth.	That clue changes my picture. Maybe it's a shark. They live in the water and have sharp teeth.
It begins with the letter *a*.	The letter *a* means the word must begin with that letter. It can't be shark because it begins with the *sh* sound. Let me try to think of an animal that lives in the water that begins with *a*. I think the answer could be alligator. It begins with the correct letter, has very sharp teeth, and hides in the water.

4. Continue with another example and invite student predictions. You might ask students to name something that begins with the letter *t*. Students might suggest *turkey, table, tiger, toad, turtle,* and *tree*. Then give another clue: It lays eggs in the sand. Students might narrow their choices to *toad* or *turtle*. Finally, provide a clue that enables students to infer the anticipated answer: It has a shell on its back. Help students understand how the clues are used to make predictions, make inferences, and draw conclusions.

5. Use some other examples from *I Spy With My Little Eye*. Younger students will enjoy seeing the tab on the book pulled for a particular letter to reveal the animal described. For older students, the clues can be used without the visuals. Even though the book is intended for younger students, the clues can challenge older students. Several more challenging examples are listed below.

Example 1	*Example 2*
Catches flies	Black and white
Has a very long tongue	Very small when born
Is a lizard	Loves eating bamboo shoots
Begins with the letter *i*	Begins with the letter *p*
(iguana)	(panda)
Example 3	*Example 4*
Small and green	Lives in the countryside
Lives in a pond	Lays eggs you can eat
Begins with the letter *n*	Begins with the letter *q*
(newt)	(quail)

6. Invite students to provide other examples. Encourage students to give reasons for their thinking. They might also want to play I Spy with a partner to help refine their skills at prediction and drawing conclusions.

7. Look for additional opportunities in materials students read to foster mental images from the text. Students can also be invited to share especially powerful passages from their independent reading.

References

Gambrell, L. B., & Koskinen, P. (2002). Imagery: A strategy for enhancing comprehension. In C. C. Block & M. Pressley (Eds.), *Comprehension instruction: Research-based best practices* (pp. 305–318). New York: Guilford.

Gardner, L. (2001). *I spy with my little eye*. Carlsbad, CA: Penton Kids.

Zeigler, L. L., & Johns, J. L. (2005). *Visualization: Using mental images to strengthen comprehension*. Dubuque, IA: Kendall/Hunt.

Putting Clues Together

Here is a picture of what the title looks like in my imagination.

Here's what I picture from my reading.

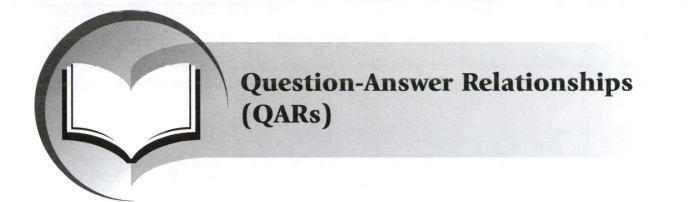

Question-Answer Relationships (QARs)

FOCUS		TEXT		WHEN			WHY									HOW			
Comprehension	Vocabulary	Narrative	Informational	Before Reading	During Reading	After Reading	Predicting	Connecting	Questioning	Using Text Structure	Visualizing	Inferring	Summarizing	Synthesizing	Determining Importance	Individual	Partner	Small Group	Whole Group
•		•	•	•		•	•	•	•	•		•		•		•			•

DESCRIPTION

Question-Answer Relationships (QARs), developed by Raphael (1982, 1984, 1986), is a strategy to help students identify the different sources of information for answering questions. It also gives students language to use in talking about the strategy (Raphael & Au, 2005). The National Reading Panel (2000) supports the answering of questions as one way to help strengthen comprehension. Although designed for students in the middle and upper grades, QARs are also an effective questioning strategy for younger students. There are four kinds of questions in QARs. Two of the question types are subsumed in a category called In the Book: Right There (students find the answer within a single sentence) and Think and Search (students need to piece together information from one or more texts). The other category of questions is called In My Head which is further divided into Author and Me and On My Own. Author and Me questions ask students to consider the author's perspective and/or position along with their own experiences to formulate a response. On My Own questions invite students to make a personal connection or evaluation related to something they have experienced or are experiencing. Using graphics in this lesson greatly aids the teaching and understanding of QARs.

Teaching Goals

1. To improve students' abilities to answer questions.
2. To help students understand and analyze the task demands of questions.
3. To strengthen students' comprehension, test-taking skills, and ability to apply higher-level thinking to text.

Procedure

QARs are best taught over several days and practiced on a regular basis. For this reason, four different lessons are presented. They should be adapted to meet the needs of your students.

Lesson 1

1. It is helpful to have charts or overhead transparencies showing the separate types of QARs as well as their relationships to each other. The graphics that follow are also available on pages 162–163. It is wise to limit the initial lesson to In the Book QARs. To introduce the concept of QARs, you might say the following.

    I want to help you learn about different kinds of questions and the best way to answer them. Take a look at the chart on the overhead projector. [Students may also be given a copy of the chart.] QARs stands for Question-Answer Relationships. That means that there is a relationship or connection between a question and where to find the answer. Let's find out about the different kinds of QARs.

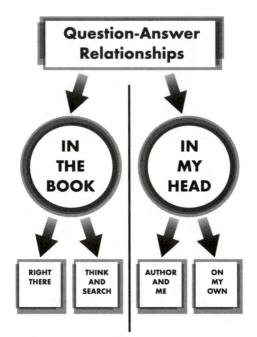

2. Focus on the first type of In the Book QAR. You might say the following.

    Look at the circle where it says In the Book. Under the circle are two types or kinds of questions: Right There and Think and Search. The answer to a Right There question is right there in a book. It can be found in one place in a book or text.

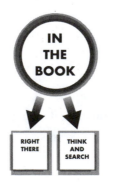

3. Show the Right There graphic on the overhead projector or display it chart form. Use an actual example from classroom materials to illustrate this type of QAR or a simple sentence like *The cat ran to the door.* Ask "What ran?" and "Where did the cat run?" and have students answer the questions and point to where the answer can be found. Ask students to name this type of QAR.

4. Continue with the Think and Search QAR in a manner similar to that above. You could say the following.

   You can see that there a second kind of QAR related to In the Book. What is it? [Think and Search]. To answer this type of question, you have to put or piece together information from different parts of the book or text.

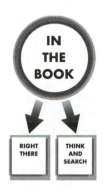

5. Show the Think and Search graphic on the overhead projector or display it in chart form. Be sure students understand that the answer comes from different parts of the book. It may not be on the same page. The answer may also use different words than the message in the text. In addition, sometimes the answer may come from two different texts. Provide an example to help illustrate this type of QAR. For example, *The cat ran to the door. Then the cat began to meow.* Ask "What did the cat do?" Have students answer the question. Be sure to note that the answer is not in one place and that students will need to do some thinking and searching.

6. Use other examples from classroom materials where students must search more than a single page to find the answer. Have students identify this type of QAR.

7. Create opportunities for students to practice what you have taught. Use passages composed of two or three sentences. You can create the passages or find them in classroom materials. Develop questions for the passages. Give the passages and questions to students along with identifying the QAR in words. Discuss the answers and make connections to the passages. Below are examples.

   Rosa and Kim were great friends. They walked to school together.

    What were Rosa and Kim?

   great friends _____

   Billy likes ice cream. Marie likes apples. Kim likes milk.

    What do Billy, Marie, and Kim like?

   ice cream, apples, and milk _____

8. Provide a second opportunity for students to practice. Give students passages, questions, and correct answers to the questions. Students, as a group, should identify the type of QAR for each question. Clarify student responses as needed.

9. A final stage of practice involves passages and questions. Students should read the passages, determine the QARs, and write the answers. Ample time should be spent in having students think aloud to explain their reasoning.

Lesson 2

1. Review the first lesson. Then teach the two types of In My Head QARs. Use a procedure similar to Lesson 1. In addition, provide practice opportunities that extend the learning to include all four types of QARs. Be sure to use examples and materials that are of interest to your students. The remaining part of this lesson will highlight the general procedure. Refer to ideas from Lesson 1 as needed and transfer them to this lesson.

2. Tell students that they will be learning about more QARs. Present the chart in the classroom or on the overhead projector and say the following.

> You have been learning about the two kinds of QARs that are In the Book. [Review them briefly.] Today we will learn about the QARs that are In My Head. Who can tell me one of them? [Invite a student to respond.] That's right. It's called Author and Me. You know that the author is the person who writes the material or book. Sometimes you are asked to use information from the author along with information already in your head to make an answer. What you already know in your head can be used to help you answer the question. [Make sure that students know that their background knowledge is a relevant source in answering these types of questions. Use an example from your classroom materials and model the process for students.]

3. Continue with a description of the On My Own type of question. You could say the following.

> Now let's look at the last kind of QAR. It's called On My Own. The answer is not in the text. You need to use your own ideas and experiences to answer the question. Before reading, I could ask what you already know about a certain topic. Your answer would come from your previous knowledge and experience. Suppose we read a story about a person who is very excited. I could ask, "What do you do when you are excited?" You could answer even though you have not read the story. [Provide additional examples so students can express feelings and understandings.]

4. Create or use materials to provide practice along the lines of Lesson 1. Proceed in a systematic and intentional manner in order to help solidify and extend student learning.

Lesson 3

1. The focus of this lesson is to provide passages of 75–150 words so students can practice QARs in a natural reading situation.

2. Review each QAR category using the QAR chart or a transparency on an overhead projector. Then present the passage and five questions that use the various QARs. It is useful to do the first passage as a group and provide feedback and guidance as necessary.

3. Provide a second passage and questions that students complete independently. Engage students in discussion to justify their answers and the QAR identified. If necessary, explain why a particular answer is acceptable. In some cases, students may be able to justify more than one answer.

4. Use a similar procedure with subsequent passages.

Lesson 4 and Beyond

1. Tell students that these lessons are practice opportunities using passages that approximate the length of students' typical reading.

2. Select a passage approximately the length of a short story. Divide the passage into four sections and create two questions for each QAR with the exception of On My Own. Have students identify the QAR type and answer the question.

3. Use the first section as a way to review and reinforce the strategy. Students should complete the remaining three sections independently.

4. Have students share their responses to each of the three sections. Provide rich opportunities for discussion and interaction. Provide appropriate feedback as needed.

5. Subsequent lessons should provide opportunities to use QARs with both narrative and informational passages read in their entirety. Depending on the length of the passage, create up to six questions for Right There, Think and Search, and Author and Me (a total of 18 questions). Students should read the passage independently, determine the QAR for each question, and answer the questions. Class discussion and appropriate feedback and guidance should be provided. Spend ample time discussing the questions and the kind of thinking involved in answering them. It can help students realize different levels of thinking and the role of text background knowledge and experience. Students should gain greater awareness of their thinking processes or metacognition.

Additional Tips for Using QARs
Raphael, 1986

1. Too many Right There QARs may indicate an overemphasis on literal, detail questions.

2. Think and Search QARs should dominate because they require integration of information and should build to asking Author and Me QARs.

3. On My Own QARs are designed to help students think about what they already know and how it relates to an upcoming story or content text. They can also be used after reading to help students react (For example, Would you like to be a biologist?)

4. For extension activities, create primarily On My Own or Author and Me QARs to help focus on students' background information as it pertains to the text.

5. QARs initially help students understand that information from both texts and their knowledge base is important to consider when answering questions.

6. QARs can help students determine text structures in informational text (compare/contrast, cause/effect, list/example, explanation).

7. QARs help students realize that some information for a question may not be in the text, and it is necessary to read between or beyond the lines to draw appropriate conclusions and inferences.

References

National Reading Panel (2000). *Teaching children to read: An evidence-based assessment of the scientific research literature on reading and its implications for reading instruction*. Washington, DC: National Institute for Child Health & Human Development.

Raphael, T. E. (1982). Question-answering strategies for children. *The Reading Teacher, 36,* 186–190.

Raphael, T. E. (1984). Teaching learners about sources of information for answering comprehension questions. *Journal of Reading, 27,* 303–311.

Raphael, T. E. (1986). Teaching question-answer relationships, revisited. *The Reading Teacher, 39,* 516–522.

Raphael, T. E. & Au, K. H. (2005). QAR: Enhancing comprehension and test taking across grades and contact areas. *The Reading Teacher, 59,* 206–221

Question-Answer Relationships

IN THE BOOK

IN MY HEAD

RIGHT THERE

THINK AND SEARCH

AUTHOR AND ME

ON MY OWN

Question-Answer Relationships (QARs)

IN THE BOOK

Right There

It's right there! The answer to this question can be found in one place in the text.

Think and Search

To arrive at the answer to this question you need to piece together different parts of one or more texts.

IN MY HEAD

On My Own

This type of question invites you to make a personal connection to something you have experienced or are experiencing.

Author and Me

The response to this question asks you to consider the author's perspective/position and your own experiences and views to formulate a response.

Name _____

Question-Answer Relationships

□ Right There
□ Think and Search
□ Author and Me
□ On My Own

Question: _____

Answer: _____
_____

□ Right There
□ Think and Search
□ Author and Me
□ On My Own

Question: _____

Answer: _____
_____

164

Questioning the Author

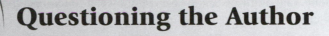

FOCUS		TEXT		WHEN			WHY									HOW			
Comprehension	Vocabulary	Narrative	Informational	Before Reading	During Reading	After Reading	Predicting	Connecting	Questioning	Using Text Structure	Visualizing	Inferring	Summarizing	Synthesizing	Determining Importance	Individual	Partner	Small Group	Whole Group
•		•	•		•				•			•	•			•	•	•	•

DESCRIPTION

As students read, they need to be actively engaged in thinking about the meanings of the text. Students often read books, especially informational passages, without asking themselves the questions that would facilitate comprehension. A strategy that promotes comprehension through questioning during reading is Questioning the Author (Beck, McKeown, Hamilton, & Kucan, 1997). The idea behind Questioning the Author is that once students identify authors as real people who are trying to present a message, they can actively question the authors' intentions about the message of the text. Questioning the Author will take several demonstrations before most students begin applying this strategy consistently while they read.

Teaching Goals

1. To promote students' comprehension through the use of questioning and summarizing.
2. To help students actively monitor their reading.
3. To encourage students to evaluate the clarity of the author's message.
4. To help students read like a writer.

Procedure

1. Hold up a book that you want students to read and tell students that one or more authors wrote the book. Explain to students that authors do the best job they can to express their ideas, but that sometimes authors are not very clear and that readers need to ask questions while they read. An example using the book *Pole to Pole* (Taylor, 1999) follows.

    Today we're going to read a book titled *Pole to Pole*. What do you think this book will be about? [Give students time to respond before answering. The book is about the North and South Poles.]

    What picture clues do we have that can help us predict what will be in the book? [The front cover has a picture of a wolf and a smaller picture of an ice house.]

    The author of this book is Barbara Taylor. She wrote this book to try to explain what it's like on the North and South Poles. She wrote this book for readers who had never visited either of the Poles so that we could know what it's like.

    Barbara Taylor wrote this book for children, but adults like the book too. She wanted children to understand some facts about the Poles through this book.

2. Tell students that as they read *Pole to Pole* they should determine what Barbara Taylor was trying to communicate by asking questions as if she were right next to them. Explain to students that by asking questions of the author during reading, they will develop a better understanding of the book.

3. Duplicate and distribute the reproducible master of Questioning the Author on page 168. Tell students that they should ask themselves the questions on this sheet as they read.

4. Demonstrate how you would use the Questioning the Author sheet with a book of your choosing or use the example that follows.

    As I read from *Pole to Pole*, I was interested in the way the author organized the print. The pages are organized like a website or an encyclopedia. The organization made the book easier for me to read.

    One of the sections of the book that I liked best was on pages 10 and 11, Arctic Animals. I'll ask myself the questions using that part. Since there is only one author, I'll question the author rather than authors.

    The first question is, "What is the author trying to say here?" I think Barbara Taylor is trying to explain about the different animals in the arctic. She has paragraphs on seals, the arctic fritillary butterfly, walruses, auks, lemmings, and wolves.

    "Why did the author include these passages?" I think she wanted her readers to know a little bit about a few of the animals found at the North Pole. She lists some of the other birds and animals that live at the North Pole, one of which is a musk ox. I wish she had written about that animal.

    "Does the author explain things clearly?" Yes, she writes very clearly.

    "Is the author good at writing for children?" The book might have too many details for some children, but the illustrations make the book easy to read.

    "What could the author have done to make the book easier to understand?" Some of the sentences are pretty long and hard to follow. Shorter sentences might help.

    "In what ways is the author effective?" Barbara Taylor was able to get me to read all about the North and South Poles and to remember lots of information about both of them. The things she chose to write about were really interesting. She's a good writer.

5. Have students select a partner. Then ask students to read another section from the book you were modeling. Have one student pretend to be the author and the other one pretend to be the reader. Have students Question the Author through role playing.

6. After students have had several experiences role playing Questioning the Author, encourage students to ask the questions independently. They might ask the questions silently or they could write answers to questions on the accompanying reproducibles on pages 168–169.

7. Remind students to ask questions frequently while they read.

References

Beck, I. L., McKeown, M. G., Hamilton, R. L., & Kucan, L. (1997). *Questioning the author: An approach for enhancing student engagement with text.* Newark, DE: International Reading Association.

Taylor, B. (1999). *Pole to pole.* Hauppauge, NY: Barron's.

Name _____ Date _____

Questioning the Author

_____
Title

1. Who is the author of this book?

   _____

2. Do you think the author did a good job writing this book for readers like you? Why or why not?

   _____

   _____

   _____

   _____

   _____

3. What would you do differently if you were the author of this book?

   _____

   _____

   _____

   _____

   _____

   _____

Name _____ Date _____

 **Questioning the Author**

_____
Title

1. What is the author trying to say here? _____

_____

_____

_____

2. Why did the author include this passage or example? _____

_____

_____

3. Did the author explain things clearly? _____

_____

_____

4. Is the author good at writing for children? Why or why not? _____

_____

_____

5. What could the author have done to make this easier to understand? _____

_____

_____

6. In what ways did the author do a good job? _____

_____

_____

_____

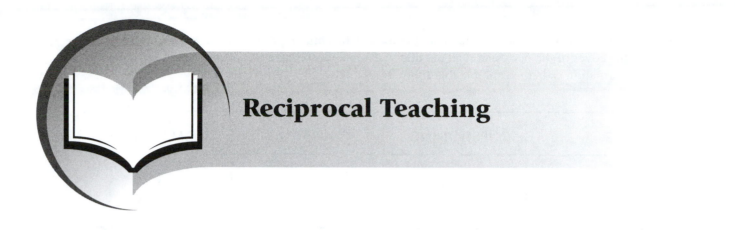

Reciprocal Teaching

FOCUS		TEXT		WHEN			WHY									HOW			
Comprehension	Vocabulary	Narrative	Informational	Before Reading	During Reading	After Reading	Predicting	Connecting	Questioning	Using Text Structure	Visualizing	Inferring	Summarizing	Synthesizing	Determining Importance	Individual	Partner	Small Group	Whole Group
•		•	•	•	•	•	•	•	•				•	•	•	•	•	•	•

DESCRIPTION

Reciprocal teaching was developed by Brown and Palincsar (1984) as a way to improve reading comprehension through active thinking. Reciprocal Teaching helps students refine four different comprehension strategies: questioning, clarifying, summarizing, and predicting.

Teaching Goals

1. To encourage students to use questioning, clarifying, summarizing, and predicting as they read.
2. To provide students with practice on asking and answering questions about text.
3. To help students improve their comprehension by incorporating more than one strategy at a time.

Procedure

1. Select an unfamiliar narrative or informational book or passage for students to read such as *Qu'Appelle* by David Brouchard (2002). This book is a legend that takes place in the Qu'Appelle Valley in Canada.

2. Duplicate and distribute copies of the blank Reciprocal Teaching reproducible on page 175. Show students the cover of the book and read the title. Ask students to make predictions about the book based on this information as in the example that follows.

PREDICTING	QUESTIONING	CLARIFYING	SUMMARIZING
This will be a story about Native Americans.			
It's winter.			
The men are leaving their village.			
The story is set in a cold region.			

3. Read the first several pages of *Qu'Appelle* to students or have them read it in groups. Ask students to develop questions about the book that will promote their comprehension. For example, you could say the following.

> When good readers read a new passage, they make predictions about what they will be reading. We've already made some predictions. As you read, you should also ask questions about your reading that you want answered. The questions will most likely stem from the predictions you've made, but they also might come from other ideas. Here are a few questions I had as I began reading *Qu'Appelle*. I'll write them on the Reciprocal Teaching sheet.

4. Write one or two questions on the Reciprocal Teaching sheet to model the types of questions that students could ask as they read. An example follows.

PREDICTING	QUESTIONING	CLARIFYING	SUMMARIZING
	Why were the Native Americans leaving their village?		
	What does the term Qu'Appelle have to do with the story?		

5. Write the questions that students generate on the Reciprocal Teaching reproducible. Then divide the class into small groups. Have students select one or more questions to discuss in their groups.

6. After students have discussed the questions, explain to students that sometimes parts of the texts are not clear and need clarification. Tell students that good readers monitor their comprehension by looking for parts that are not clear.

7. Have students discuss areas that need to be clarified in their groups. If students need parts of the story clarified, write those parts on the Reciprocal Teaching reproducible as follows.

PREDICTING	QUESTIONING	CLARIFYING	SUMMARIZING
		This book is a Canadian legend from the First Nations.	
		Qu'Appelle is French for "Who's calling?"	

8. Remind students that summarizing helps them remember what they have read. Tell students that they can summarize during reading as well as after reading. Have students summarize what they know from their reading thus far. An example follows.

PREDICTING	QUESTIONING	CLARIFYING	SUMMARIZING
			The legend tells about a voice that can be heard on the prairie. The voice calls, "Qu'Appelle," or "Who calls?" The legend is about a young warrior who comes back from a raid and finds that his young wife has died.

9. Have students practice the strategies of predicting, questioning, clarifying, and summarizing in small groups during reading. As students become adept at these strategies, have one member of the group act as the leader and guide the discussion. Rotate leaders so that each student has the opportunity of being a group member and a leader.

10. Encourage students to use the strategies of predicting, questioning, clarifying, and summarizing independently as they read.

References

Brouchard, D. (2002). *Qu'Appelle*. Vancouver, BC: Raincoat Books.

Brown, A. L., & Palincsar, A. S. (1984). Reciprocal teaching of comprehension: Fostering and monitoring activities. *Cognition and Instruction, 1,* 117–175.

Name _____ Date _____

Title _____

Reciprocal Teaching

PREDICTING	QUESTIONING	CLARIFYING	SUMMARIZING

RIVET

FOCUS		TEXT		WHEN			WHY									HOW			
Comprehension	Vocabulary	Narrative	Informational	Before Reading	During Reading	After Reading	Predicting	Connecting	Questioning	Using Text Structure	Visualizing	Inferring	Summarizing	Synthesizing	Determining Importance	Individual	Partner	Small Group	Whole Group
	•	•	•	•			•												•

DESCRIPTION

The primary goal of teaching vocabulary strategies is for students to increase comprehension, but many students do not stay actively involved in learning during traditional vocabulary lessons. To combat inattention during vocabulary lessons, Cunningham (2005) developed the RIVET strategy. During RIVET, teachers focus students' attention on the individual letters of the new words, and students become "riveted" on the words. Using RIVET encourages the use of prior knowledge and predictions, which also fosters improved comprehension.

Teaching Goals

1. To motivate students to predict key words in a selection or unit of study.
2. To help students predict the content of a reading selection based on key vocabulary words.

Procedure

1. Identify a text that has new vocabulary terms that you would like students to be able to read. Read the text and select six to eight key words, with an emphasis on polysyllabic words and important names. For example, a list for a social studies book might include the following words.
   1. Americans
   2. Holidays
   3. Celebrate

4. Thanksgiving
5. Washington
6. Presidents
7. Memorial
8. Independence

2. Write numbers for the list of words on the board with blanks for each letter of the words. For example, if your first word is *Americans,* write number one followed by nine blanks.

   1. ___ ___ ___ ___ ___ ___ ___ ___ ___

3. Duplicate and distribute copies of the RIVET reproducible master on page 180.

4. Fill in the letters to the first word one at a time. Tell students to write the letters as you do and encourage them to predict the word as soon as they think they know it. For example, you might say the following.

   > I've selected some words from our reading today that I want you to guess. The first word has nine blanks, so it has nine letters. I'm going to write one letter at a time and ask you to predict the word. I'll stop after each letter so you can make your guesses. Please raise your hands, and I'll call on one of you as soon as your hand is up.

5. As you fill in the letters, allow ample time for guessing the word. Once a student guesses the correct word, have him or her help you finish spelling it on the board while students write it on their papers. If students guess incorrect words, just continue writing letters until someone guesses the correct word. An example follows.

   1. A m e r ___ ___ ___ ___ ___

6. Continue writing the letters of each word until all words have been guessed and written correctly on the board and on the students' papers.

7. After students have completed their list of words, ask students to make predictions about the text. Encourage as many divergent predictions as possible by asking questions leading to alternative possibilities. For example, a student might say, "Americans are people who live in the United States." A leading question following that prediction could be, "Do all Americans live in the United States?" Continue asking for predictions for each of the words.

8. During discussions, students will learn the context of the vocabulary words. To deepen students' understandings of the words, ask them to predict a definition. Discuss possible definitions for words guiding students to develop an accurate meaning for the word, as in the example of a conversation about the word *Americans* that follows.

   > Brad: Americans are people who live in the United States.

   > Miss Wilcox: Do all Americans live in the United States?

   > Samantha: There are other countries in America.

   > Miss Wilcox: What other countries can you think of?

   > José: Mexico and Canada are in North America.

   > Miss Wilcox: Yes, they are. Is there another America?

   > Maria: There's also Central America and South America.

   > Miss Wilcox: Good. Can you now tell me a definition for Americans?

George: Americans are people who live in North, Central, and South America.

Miss Wilcox: Let's write that definition on our RIVET sheet. That definition will help you as you read the social studies book today.

9. Instruct students to write the agreed upon definition or meaning on the RIVET reproducible master on page 180.

Reference

Cunningham, P. M. (2005). *Phonics they use* (4th ed.). Boston: Allyn & Bacon.

RIVET

⇛ **DIRECTIONS**

Write the letters for the vocabulary words on the blanks, with one letter for each blank. You might have some blanks left over. After class discussion, write what you think the word means on the line below each word.

1. Word __ __ __ __ __ __ __ __ __ __ __ __ __ __

   Meaning

   _____

2. Word __ __ __ __ __ __ __ __ __ __ __ __ __ __

   Meaning

   _____

3. Word __ __ __ __ __ __ __ __ __ __ __ __ __ __

   Meaning

   _____

4. Word __ __ __ __ __ __ __ __ __ __ __ __

   Meaning

   _____

5. Word __ __ __ __ __ __ __ __ __ __ __ __

   Meaning

   _____

6. Word __ __ __ __ __ __ __ __ __ __ __ __ __ __ __

   Meaning

   _____

Based on Cunningham, P. M. (2005). *Phonics they use* (4th ed.). Boston: Allyn & Bacon.

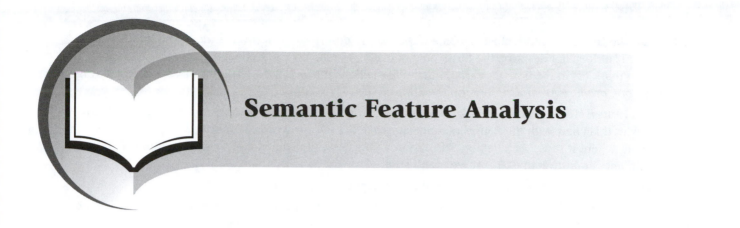

Semantic Feature Analysis

FOCUS		TEXT		WHEN			WHY									HOW			
Comprehension	Vocabulary	Narrative	Informational	Before Reading	During Reading	After Reading	Predicting	Connecting	Questioning	Using Text Structure	Visualizing	Inferring	Summarizing	Synthesizing	Determining Importance	Individual	Partner	Small Group	Whole Group
	•	•	•			•	•	•	•					•					•

DESCRIPTION

Semantic Feature Analysis (Berglund, 2002; Johnson & Pearson, 1984) is an instructional strategy that helps students understand the uniqueness of a word, as well as its relationships to other words. It uses a grid system to help students determine semantic similarities and differences among words.

Teaching Goals

1. To help students to deepen their understanding of the similarities and differences among words related to a concept or topic.
2. To enable students to visually see relationships between and among words.
3. To engage students in actively examining the shades of meaning of words.

Procedure

1. Select a text on a topic for which your students have some background knowledge.
2. Write the name of the topic on a chart, the board, or an overhead transparency. List terms related to the topic down the left side of the grid. List features or properties related to the topic across the top of the grid. See the sample on page 183 and the reproducible master on page 184.

3. Discuss the first term and feature. Decide if the feature describes the term. If it does, put a plus (+) in the box. If it does not describe the term, put a minus (–) in the box. If students are unsure, then put a question mark (?) in the box. (A variation is to use smiley and sad faces.) You might say the following about *Look at these Animals* (Christopher, 2003).

> Miss Hett: Before I read this book about animals to you, I want you to share some things you know. Look at this chart with the names of some animals. I'll say the words. [Pronounce the words.] Now look at where it says, "can be pets." Let's put a plus (+) if the animal can be a pet, a minus (–) if it can't, and a question mark (?) if we aren't sure.

> Casey: I think a dog is a mammal, and it can be a pet.

> Miss Hett: Class, do you agree? Okay, what should we put here? [Point to where "dogs" and "can be pets" intersect.]

> John: Put a plus. And you should also put a plus for birds, because I have a parakeet for a pet.

> Kari: I have a fish for a pet so put a plus there.

> Miss Hett: What about amphibians?

> Corey: I think they are dangerous so they wouldn't be pets.

> Miss Hett: I'll put a minus in that box. [See partially completed Semantic Feature Analysis Chart that follows. Complete the chart with teacher guidance, remembering that initial impressions may be incorrect.]

4. Have students read the selected text. Students might suggest any terms or features that can be added to the chart. They could also note any questions that are answered in the text.

5. Discuss the students' findings, adding appropriate information to the chart. After reading, students should discover that amphibians can also be pets, so the minus should be changed to a plus.

6. Complete additional Semantic Feature Analysis charts as a whole class activity. When students are familiar with the strategy, use or adapt the reproducible masters on pages 184–185. You may wish to use the term "Word Grid" in place of Semantic Feature Analysis.

7. You may also encourage students to draw a conclusion about the similarities and/or differences among the concepts.

References

Berglund, R. L. (2002). Semantic feature analysis. In B. J. Guzzetti (Ed.), *Literacy in America: An encyclopedia of history, theory, and practice.* (pp. 566–572). Santa Barbara, CA: ABC-CLIO.

Christopher, G. (2003). *Look at these animals.* New York: Sadlier-Oxford.

Johnson, D. D., & Pearson, P. D. (1984). *Teaching reading vocabulary* (2nd ed.). New York: Holt, Rinehart, and Winston.

Semantic Feature Analysis

Look at These Animals by G. Christopher

	FEATURES								
WORDS	CAN BE PETS	COOL, DRY SKIN	HATCH FROM EGGS	WET, COOL SKIN	SCALES	LAY EGGS	GILLS	WINGS	FUR OR HAIR
dogs	+	–	–	–	–				
birds	+	–	+	–	–				
fish	+	–	?	+	+				
amphibians	–	?	+	+	–				
reptiles	?	?	+	+	?				

Jerry L. Johns, Susan Davis Lenski, and Roberta L. Berglund. *Comprehension and Vocabulary Strategies for the Elementary Grades* (2nd ed.). Copyright © 2006 by Kendall/Hunt Publishing Company (1-800-247-3458, ext. 4).

Name _____ Date _____

Semantic Feature Analysis (SFA)

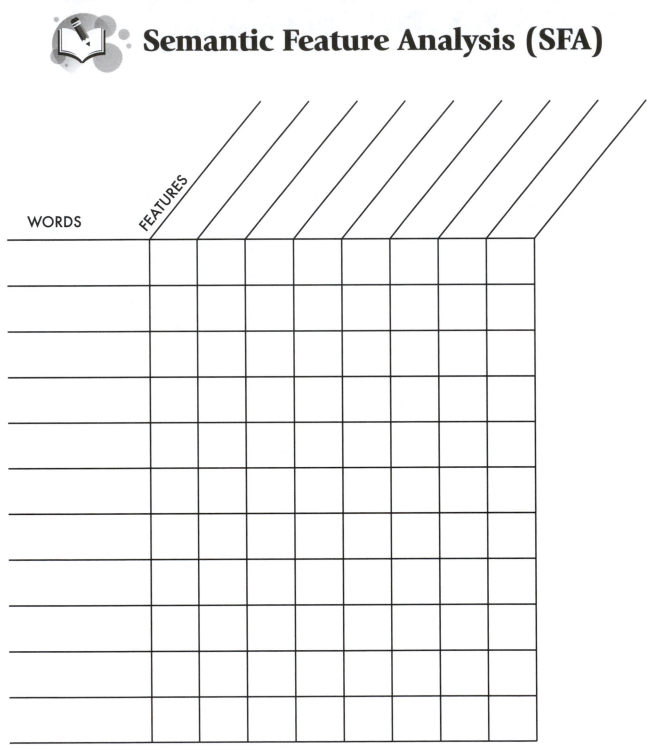

WORDS

FEATURES

Name _____ Date _____

Word Grid

WORDS	FEATURES				

Conclusion: _____
_____

Based on Berglund, R. L. (2002). Semantic feature analysis in B. J. Guzzetti (Ed.), *Literacy in America: An encyclopedia of history, theory, and practice* (pp. 566–572). Santa Barbara, CA: ABC-CLIO and Johnson, D. D., & Pearson, P. D. (1984). *Teaching reading vocabulary* (2nd ed.). New York: Holt, Rinehart, and Winston.

Jerry L. Johns, Susan Davis Lenski, and Roberta L. Berglund. *Comprehension and Vocabulary Strategies for the Elementary Grades* (2nd ed.). Copyright © 2006 by Kendall/Hunt Publishing Company (1-800-247-3458, ext. 4). May be reproduced for noncommercial educational purposes within the guidelines noted on the copyright page.

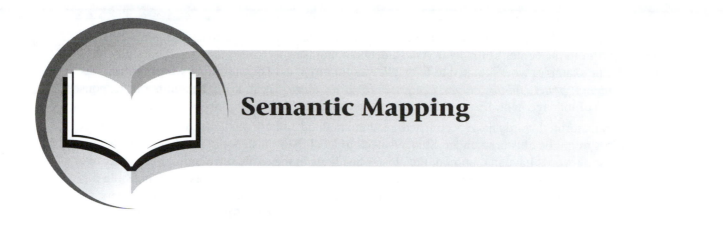

Semantic Mapping

FOCUS		TEXT		WHEN			WHY									HOW			
Comprehension	Vocabulary	Narrative	Informational	Before Reading	During Reading	After Reading	Predicting	Connecting	Questioning	Using Text Structure	Visualizing	Inferring	Summarizing	Synthesizing	Determining Importance	Individual	Partner	Small Group	Whole Group
•	•	•	•	•	•	•		•						•	•	•		•	

DESCRIPTION

Semantic Mapping (Heimlich & Pittelman, 1986; Johnson & Pearson, 1984; Pearson & Johnson, 1978) helps students to bridge what they know about a topic and what they learn from information in the text or from another information source. Semantic Mapping actively involves students in graphically organizing information in categorical form. The four-step strategy (brainstorming, categorizing, reading, and revising the categories) helps students to become active readers and, in the process, remember new vocabulary and information.

Teaching Goals

1. To help students activate and organize knowledge about a specific topic.
2. To help students graphically see relationships among words.
3. To have students classify words into superordinate and subordinate concepts.
4. To help students expand their vocabularies.

Procedure

1. Choose a major concept or topic being studied by the class. In elementary science, for example, the life cycle of the butterfly is a frequently studied topic.

2. Draw an oval on the board, an overhead transparency, or use the reproducible master on page 190. Write *butterflies* in the center of the oval. Ask students to brainstorm words related to their study of *butterflies*. For example, words related to *butterflies* might be *chrysalis, caterpillar, wings, leaves, cocoon, branches, pouch, moths, colors, egg, eaten by birds, larva*. Try to keep the number of responses to ten for ease of management. List words related to the topic on the board or an overhead transparency.

3. When the brainstormed words have been listed, read them aloud and ask students to think of headings that the words might be clustered under. Students need to label their clusters or give them titles to indicate what the words have in common. Put cluster headings in the ovals surrounding the center oval. You may wish to have students complete this step in small cooperative groups. It is often possible for some of the brainstormed words to become category headings. For example, the labels for clusters related to the life cycle of butterflies might be *How They Look, How They Change, What They Eat,* and *Enemies.*

4. Next, have students try to put the brainstormed words on lines branching from the appropriate oval, showing connections to the idea within the oval. When you and the students have completed the classification and categorization of the words, invite students to share the labels for each of their clusters and the words they have included under each heading. You may wish to record these on the board or on an overhead transparency created from the reproducible master on page 190 or 191.

5. It is important that students share their reasons for their clustering decisions. This sharing stimulates students to think of the words in a variety of ways, consider their meanings, connect them, and see relationships among the words.

6. If used as a prereading activity, ask students to then read the text and evaluate their headings and the words they have clustered together. They may need to rename some of their headings and/or rearrange some words based on additional information in the lesson.

7. If used as a postreading activity, students may want to return to the text and confirm their reasons for and accuracy of their clusters and connected words.

8. The strategy work can be extended over the course of several days as students acquire additional information about the topic. More words can be added to the clusters as students expand their knowledge and increase the connections they make between and among the words. If desired, different colored inks can be used for words added from additional sources or at different times, thus graphically illustrating the expanding knowledge base of the students and the desirability of using a variety of resources in acquiring information.

9. When the semantic maps are complete, have students work individually or in pairs to write a summary of the information in one of the clusters or write a longer piece about the topic, using each one of the clusters of information as a paragraph in a main idea-detail piece. Students may also use their completed semantic maps as study aids.

References

Heimlich, J. E., & Pittelman, S. D. (1986). *Semantic mapping: Classroom applications.* Newark, DE: International Reading Association.

Johnson, D. D., & Pearson, P. D. (1984). *Teaching reading vocabulary,* (2nd ed.). New York: Holt, Rinehart & Winston.

Pearson, P. D., & Johnson, D. D. (1978). *Teaching reading comprehension.* New York: Holt, Rinehart & Winston.

Semantic Mapping

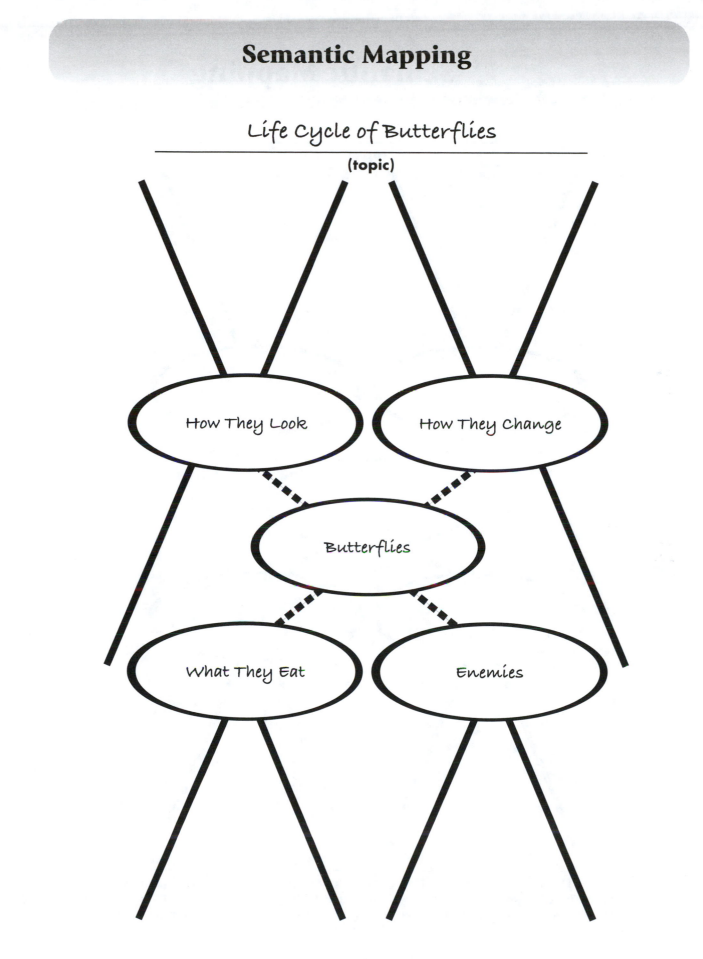

Life Cycle of Butterflies

(topic)

How They Look

How They Change

Butterflies

What They Eat

Enemies

Name _____ Date _____

Semantic Mapping

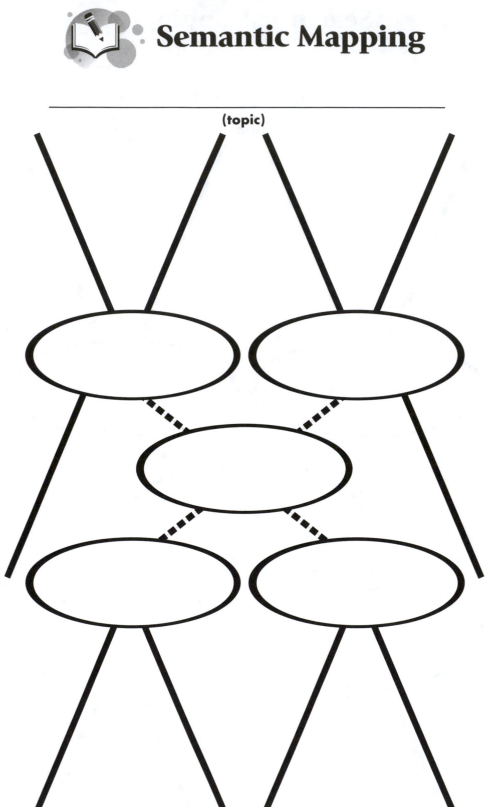

(topic)

Semantic Mapping

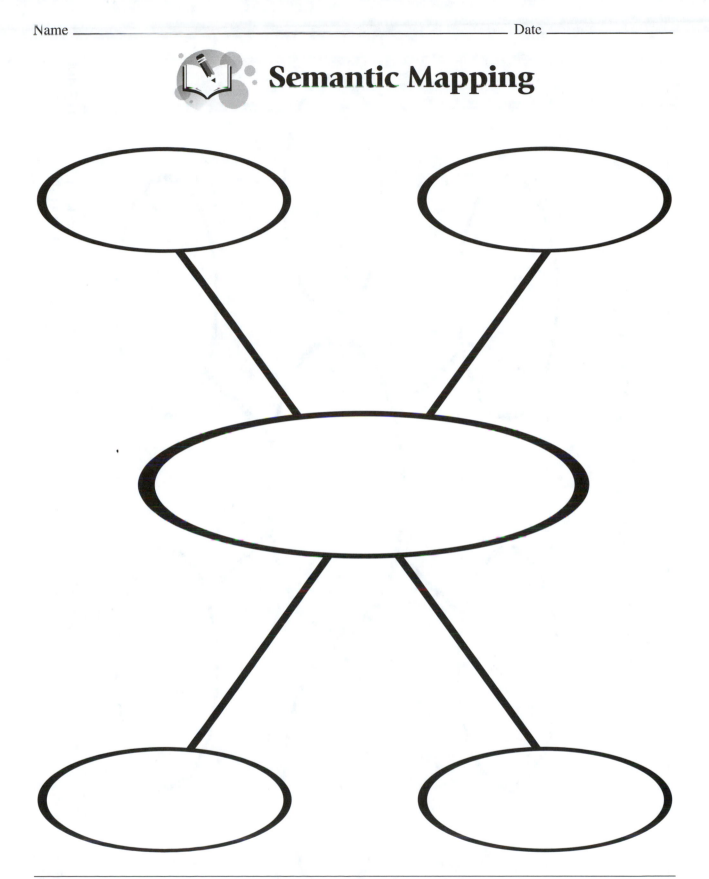

Semantic Mapping

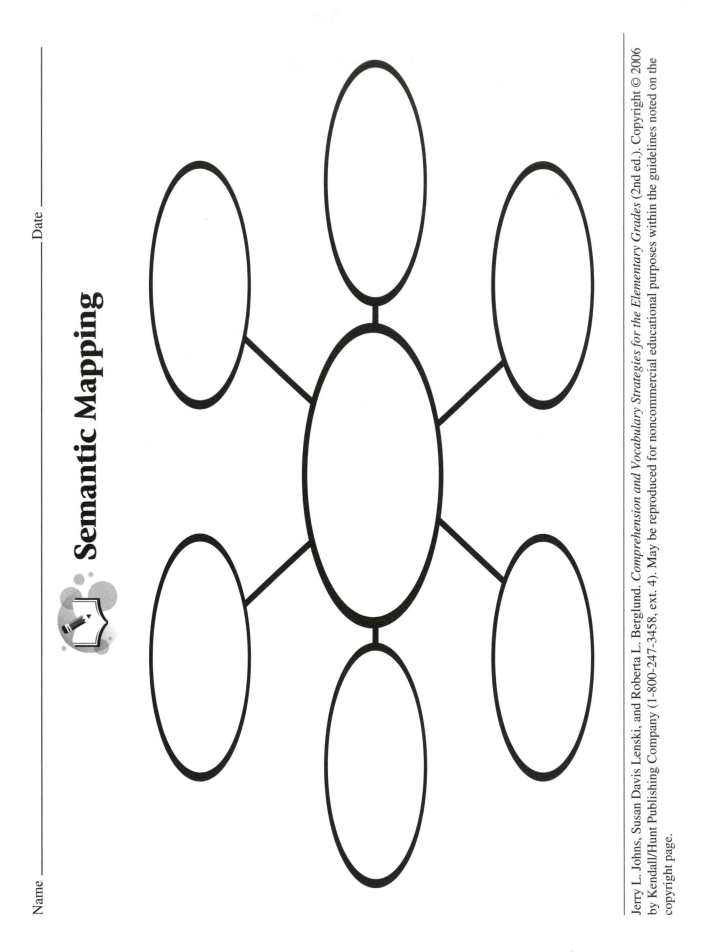

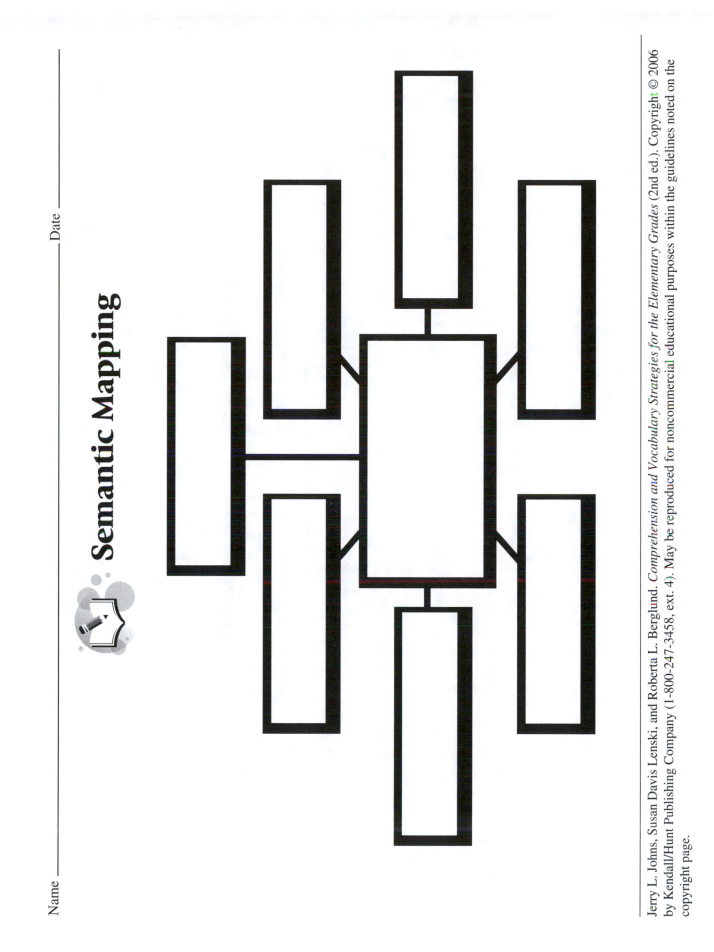

Semantic Mapping

Semantic Mapping

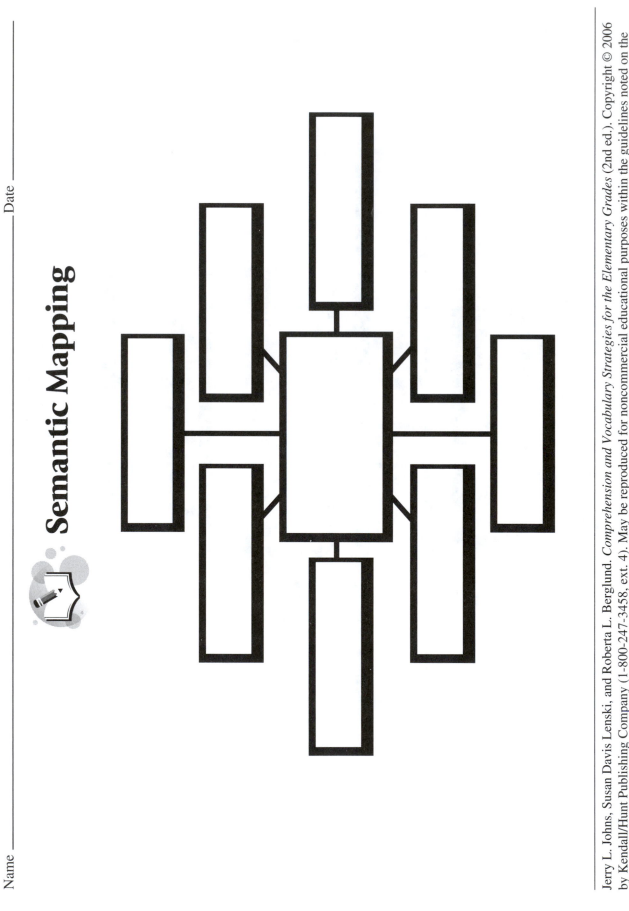

Sketch to Stretch

FOCUS		TEXT		WHEN			WHY									HOW			
Comprehension	Vocabulary	Narrative	Informational	Before Reading	During Reading	After Reading	Predicting	Connecting	Questioning	Using Text Structure	Visualizing	Inferring	Summarizing	Synthesizing	Determining Importance	Individual	Partner	Small Group	Whole Group
•		•	•			•		•			•	•					•	•	•

DESCRIPTION

Sketch to Stretch (Short, Harste, & Burke, 1996) is a strategy that offers students a way to extend meaning and respond to narrative text, informational text, or poetry following reading. Sketch to Stretch assists students in using visualization to support comprehension (McLaughlin & Allen, 2002). It also can be used as a means to help students become more comfortable in talking and working in pairs and in small groups. After students read or listen to a selection, they are asked to draw a sketch showing what the passage means to them. Sketch to Stretch can be introduced and modeled during class read-aloud experiences and can then be moved into small group settings to encourage rich discussions.

Teaching Goals

1. To extend the opportunities for students to respond after reading a selection.
2. To help students visualize emotions they feel during reading.
3. To provide students with opportunities to extend meanings from texts.

Procedure

1. Begin by reading a selected text aloud to students and modeling a think-aloud while doing so. For example, while reading aloud the informational book *Apes!* (Harrison, 1999), you might say the following.

   > As I look at this book, I am thinking, I wonder what we might learn about apes. The drawing on the cover looks very real to me, so I think this book might give me information about apes. I don't think it is going to be a make-believe story. [Read the first page: They run and wrestle. They're very curious. And they love to play just like you! They're apes!]

   > Hmmm, this sounds a lot like our recess time! Maybe apes are more like humans than I thought. As we read the rest of this book, I wonder if we are going to learn more about how apes are like us? The illustrator has drawn some pictures to help us understand more about apes, and I am going to be making some pictures in my mind as I read.

2. After finishing the read-aloud and think-aloud, introduce the idea of making a drawing of the ideas or feelings you have about the text. You might say the following.

   > I am going to do my best to sketch what I was thinking as I read. When I finish, I want you to guess what you think I was remembering and thinking about. I am not going to color my picture or make it ready to hang on the bulletin board in our artist's corner. I am just going to keep my sketch in my journal to help me remember something about the book, how I felt about it, or a connection I made with it.

3. After several students have had a chance to hypothesize about your interpretation of the text, you might say the following.

   > I drew a sketch of a gorilla with a happy expression holding a kitten because I remember learning about Koko the gorilla who had a pet kitten and actually named it! I will use this sketch to help me remember that apes have feelings and can communicate through expressions and sounds. My sketch also helps me think about whether it is right to keep apes in zoos behind bars. How would we like that? So my sketch shows me one idea I got from the book, a connection I made with something I already knew about, and it helps me remember how I felt when I read about the apes.

   > Remember, we don't need to be great artists or illustrators to sketch a picture after we read to help us remember what we read about or how it made us feel. Sketches like mine are another way we can make connections with our reading and learning. Each of us may read the same text, but our sketches may be very different. One isn't right and another one wrong. We all have different interests and backgrounds, so how we interpret the same texts may be quite different.

4. Give students an opportunity to draw sketches of their ideas about the *Apes!* book on the Sketch to Stretch reproducible from page 198.

5. After students have drawn their sketches, ask them to write what the sketch was about, how they felt about the sketch, and connections they made from the text to their sketches. Students may want to share their ideas in small groups after writing.

6. When students have finished their sketches, invite each person to show his or her sketch. Before the artist can say what the sketch is about, other students need to share their hypotheses about the sketch. Finally, it is the artist's turn to explain the sketch and how it helps the artist to connect with the text or with a feeling about it. (You may want to use the Save the Last Word for the Artist on page 199 to help guide students through the sharing process).

7. Continue sharing sketches until most students have shared or until students understand the procedures for Sketch to Stretch.

8. Explain to students that they will be using Sketch to Stretch in their small group or partner time and that they will need to remember to follow the ideas for Save the Last Word for the Artist (see page 199) when they get in their groups or work with a partner.

References

Harrison, C. (1999). *Apes!* New York: McClanahan.

McLaughlin, M., & Allen, M. B. (2002). *Guided comprehension: A teaching model for grades 3–8*. Newark, DE: International Reading Association.

Short, K. G., Harste, J. C., & Burke, C. (1996). *Creating classrooms for authors and inquirers* (2nd ed.). Portsmouth, NH: Heinemann.

Sketch to Stretch

Title ——

```




```

This sketch is about ————————————————————————————————

——

——

I feel ——

——

——

I made a connection to ——————————————————————————————

——

——

Save the Last Word for the Artist

1. Choose someone to begin.

2. Have the first person show his or her sketch without saying anything about it.

3. Take turns. Have each person say something like this about the sketch.

    I think this sketch is about . . .

    I think the artist feels . . .

    I think the artist has made a connection with . . .

4. When each person has had a chance to say something about the sketch, it is the artist's turn to talk.

5. The artist should say something like this:

    My sketch is about . . .

    My sketch shows how I felt when . . .

    My sketch shows how I made a connection to . . .

6. The next member of the group should share his or her sketch.

7. Keep sharing sketches until everyone has had a turn.

8. Now, pick one sketch from your group to share with the class.

Jerry L. Johns, Susan Davis Lenski, and Roberta L. Berglund. *Comprehension and Vocabulary Strategies for the Elementary Grades* (2nd ed.). Copyright © 2006 by Kendall/Hunt Publishing Company (1-800-247-3458, ext. 4). May be reproduced for noncommercial educational purposes within the guidelines noted on the copyright page.

Name _____ Date _____

 **Sketch to Stretch**

SKETCH	DESCRIPTION

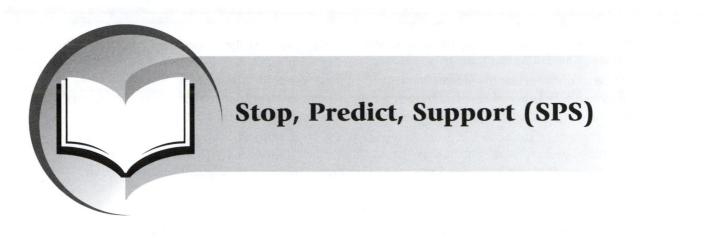

Stop, Predict, Support (SPS)

FOCUS		TEXT		WHEN			WHY									HOW			
Comprehension	Vocabulary	Narrative	Informational	Before Reading	During Reading	After Reading	Predicting	Connecting	Questioning	Using Text Structure	Visualizing	Inferring	Summarizing	Synthesizing	Determining Importance	Individual	Partner	Small Group	Whole Group
•		•	•	•	•	•	•	•					•			•	•	•	•

DESCRIPTION

The Stop, Predict, Support (SPS) strategy encourages students to use text to support the predictions they make during reading. When some students read, they make predictions from their imaginations that are not text-based. The SPS strategy invites students to use text to make predictions rather than making predictions from their imaginations alone.

Teaching Goals

1. To encourage students to make predictions while reading.
2. To invite students to use text that supports their predictions.
3. To encourage students to reflect on the predictions that they make.
4. To help students understand how knowledge of text structure assists comprehension.

Procedure

1. To introduce this strategy, identify a book or book chapter that you can read with students that has an element of suspense. (Most students find that making predictions is easier with narrative texts. Once they are comfortable with the strategy, you can use it with informational texts.) Read the book before the lesson and select three places to stop and make predictions.

2. Write the title of the book on the top of the Stop, Predict, Support (SPS) chart as in the example of *Orphan Train* (Kay, 2003) that follows.

3. Read the title of the selection to students showing them the cover of the book. Model ways to use information about the title and cover as support for predictions. Ask students to make predictions about the contents of the book by using the words in the title as in the following example.

> Teacher: The title of the book I'm going to read to you is *Orphan Train*. It was written by Verla Kay and illustrated by Ken Stark. You can see that the picture on the front cover shows a train with children waving from the windows. Let's look for information about the title and cover before we make predictions. What do you notice about the cover?
>
> Student: The train is an old one, not like trains today.
>
> Teacher: Yes, the train is not modern. What can we predict about the setting of the story based on that information?
>
> Student: The story takes place long ago.
>
> Teacher: That prediction is based on information. We call that support for your prediction. Let's try to make more predictions and discuss how they are supported.

4. Distribute blank copies of the SPS chart on page 205 to students. Write the words *prediction* and *support* on the board. Tell students that they will be making predictions about the story and that their predictions must have support. Review with students what it means to make predictions about stories. Then tell students that support means to tell *why* they made predictions. Emphasize that their reasons for predictions must be based on the content or illustrations from the story. To explain support, you might say something like the following:

> I know all of you make predictions when you read. We've used prediction charts earlier in the year. Sometimes when you made predictions, I've asked you why you make that prediction. Some of your predictions were made based on things you knew. For example, when we read *31 Uses for a Mom* (Ziefert, 2003), you made predictions based on the things your mother did for you at home. You didn't make predictions based on the story. Today, though, I'd like you to explain your predictions based on things you heard from the story that I'm going to read to you.

5. Read up to the first stopping place in the story you have selected for this lesson. After reading, point out the STOP sign on the SPS chart. Tell students that the STOP sign is there to remind them to stop while reading and make predictions.

6. Demonstrate how to make predictions using text as a support. Show students an example of a prediction and text support as in the example based on *Orphan Train* that follows. Read the first prediction.

> Prediction: The children will be taken to an orphanage.
>
> Support: The story says that the parents were sick and died and that the children were begging on the streets. Then the story says that the children were stealing for food.

7. Read the next section of the story and continue modeling making predictions with the support of the text. Use the sample on page 204 to demonstrate this strategy.

8. After you have modeled SPS with predictions and support that you have provided, ask students if they understand what it means to support their predictions with text. Demonstrate SPS using your own predictions and support as necessary. Work collaboratively with the students to make predictions and support them using the SPS strategy.

9. Once students understand the process of SPS, *have them make predictions and support using the SPS strategy with you.* Select a book for students to stop and make predictions. Ask students to write their predictions on the SPS chart. Then have students identify the text segment that supports their predictions and write that support on the chart. Provide assistance as needed.

10. Provide guidance until students are able to use the SPS strategy to make predictions with text support independently. You can use the SPS strategy with narrative and informational texts. Once students are able to support their predictions, give them the SPS chart to use during independent reading.

11. Remind students that the SPS strategy is one that they should use whenever they read. Tell students that they should make predictions using the text to support the predictions whenever they read at home or at school.

12. Blank SPS reproducibles are on pages 205–206.

References

Kay, V. (2003). *Orphan train*. New York: G. P. Putnam's Sons.

Ziefert, H. (2003). *31 uses for a Mom*. New York: G. P. Putnam's Sons.

Name _____ Date _____

Title ___Orphan Train_____

 # Stop, Predict, Support

PREDICTION	SUPPORT
STOP The children will be taken to an orphanage.	Title is <u>Orphan Train.</u> Parents died. The children were homeless and hungry.
STOP Lucy, Harold, and David will be separated.	David is taken first. All of the children are going to homes.
STOP Lucy will find a home.	Lucy is crying. A farmer's wife is looking at her. All of the children have homes.

Name _____ Date _____

Title _____

 # Stop, Predict, Support

PREDICTION	SUPPORT
STOP	
STOP	
STOP	

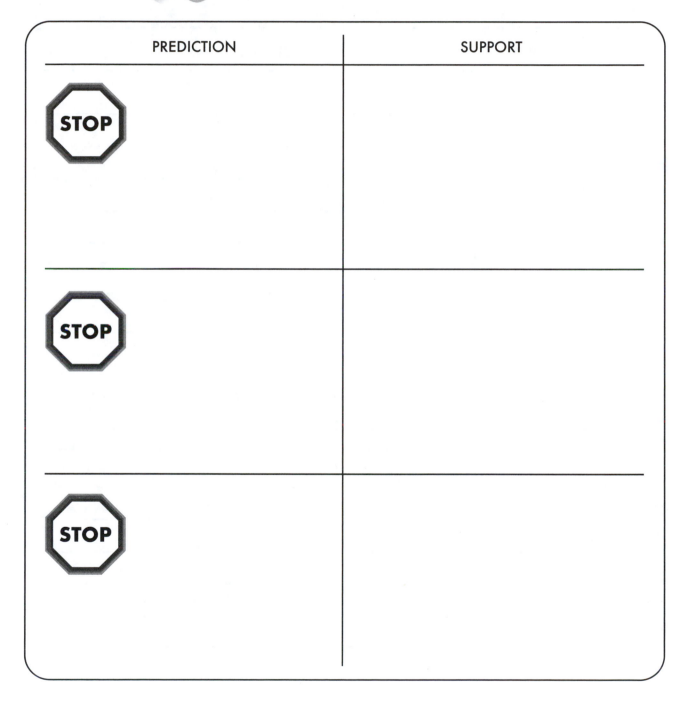

Name _____ Date _____

Title _____

Stop, Predict, Support

STOP AND PREDICT	SUPPORT
1. Page _____ _____ _____ _____ _____	_____ _____ _____ _____ _____
2. Page _____ _____ _____ _____ _____	_____ _____ _____ _____ _____
3. Page _____ _____ _____ _____	_____ _____ _____ _____

Story Board

FOCUS		TEXT		WHEN			WHY									HOW			
Comprehension	Vocabulary	Narrative	Informational	Before Reading	During Reading	After Reading	Predicting	Connecting	Questioning	Using Text Structure	Visualizing	Inferring	Summarizing	Synthesizing	Determining Importance	Individual	Partner	Small Group	Whole Group
•		•	•			•				•	•		•		•	•	•	•	•

DESCRIPTION

A Story Board is a series of frames that can be used to outline a narrative or informational text. Story Boards can show events in a series and can be written and/or illustrated. Students read or listen to a story and determine the beginning, middle, and end or the events that take place in the plot. Story Boards can help students learn how texts are organized.

Teaching Goals

1. To help students understand that narrative texts have a beginning, middle, and end.
2. To help students identify the events that take place in the plot of a narrative story.
3. To help students identify the sequence of details in informational text.

Procedure

1. Identify a story that has a clear beginning, middle, and end or that has events in a series that can be easily discerned. An example of such a story is *Beyond the Ridge* (Goble, 1989). This story tells of a Plains Indian grandmother who is dying.

2. Teach students about the organization of narrative texts. Younger students should learn that narratives have a beginning, middle, and end. Students who understand those basic concepts can learn that stories

have events that take place in order. If you are using Story Boards for informational text, you can discuss what students learn first, second, third, and so on.

3. Read the story or have students read the story in groups. As students are listening to the story, have them think about the events that occurred.

4. Provide students with a blank copy of the Story Board on page 210 or 212. One group of three frames is sufficient for students who are drawing a beginning, middle, and end. Students who are drawing a series of events should be given more than one set of frames.

5. Guide students to think about the beginning of the story as in the example that follows.

> Teacher: We are introduced to the grandmother at the beginning of the story. What happens at this point in *Beyond the Ridge?*
>
> Student: The grandmother is sick and possibly dying.
>
> Teacher: Yes, that seems to be the first part of the story. Let's consider what we learn from the rest of the story before drawing the beginning on the Story Board. What else happens in the story?
>
> Student: The grandmother hears the voice of her mother and goes to the place in the sky beyond the ridge. I think they called it the Land of Many Tipis.
>
> Teacher: What else happens?
>
> Student: The family mourns her death and gives her food for her journey.
>
> Teacher: Now we have a beginning for the story, a middle, and an end. Draw each of these events in the frames of the Story Board.

6. Have students draw a picture of the beginning of the story. Older students can write under the illustration.

7. Guide students in determining the middle and end of the story. Ask them to illustrate these parts of the story and to label or write sentences about them. Older students can write several events that occurred in the story. Make sure students write them in the order that occurred in the book.

8. Have students share their Story Boards with others in the class.

9. Remind students that narrative texts have a beginning, middle, and end and include a series of events.

10. Once students understand how to develop a Story Board with a narrative text, show how they can be used with informational text as in the example using the book *Mice* (Harper & Randell, 1997) on page 211 and by saying the following.

> I was reading the book *Mice,* and I noticed that I can also use a Story Board for an informational book. The book has sections that would fit really well on the Story Board. I can draw a picture of what mice look like in the first section, pet mice in the second section, and mice and their babies in the third section. Story Boards work really well to help organize informational text.

11. Model the use of Story Boards with informational text several times before asking students to use them independently.

12. Reproducible Story Board masters are provided on pages 210 and 212.

References

Goble, P. (1989). *Beyond the ridge.* New York: Aladdin.

Harper, C., & Randell, B. (1997). *Mice.* Nelson Price Milburn: New Zealand.

Name _____ Date _____

Title *Beyond the Ridge*

Story Board (Narrative Text)

BEGINNING	MIDDLE	END

Name _____ Date _____

Title _____

Story Board (Narrative Text)

BEGINNING	MIDDLE	END

Name _____ Date _____

Title *Mice*

Story Board (Informational Text)

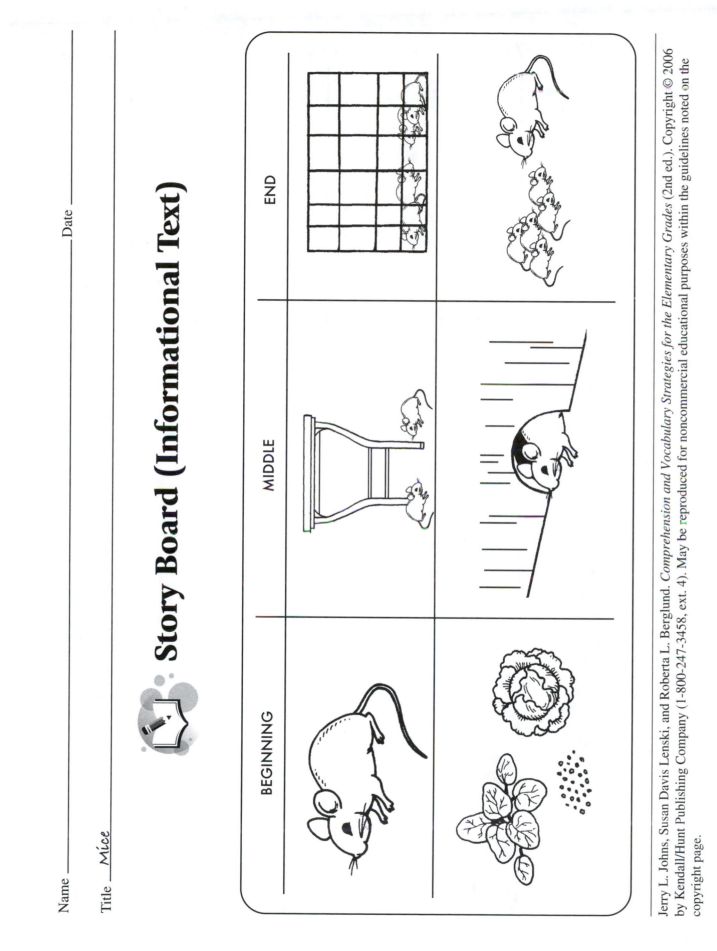

BEGINNING	MIDDLE	END

Name _____ Date _____

Title _____

Story Board (Informational Text)

BEGINNING	MIDDLE	END

Jerry L. Johns, Susan Davis Lenski, and Roberta L. Berglund. *Comprehension and Vocabulary Strategies for the Elementary Grades* (2nd ed.). Copyright © 2006 by Kendall/Hunt Publishing Company (1-800-247-3458, ext. 4). May be reproduced for noncommercial educational purposes within the guidelines noted on the copyright page.

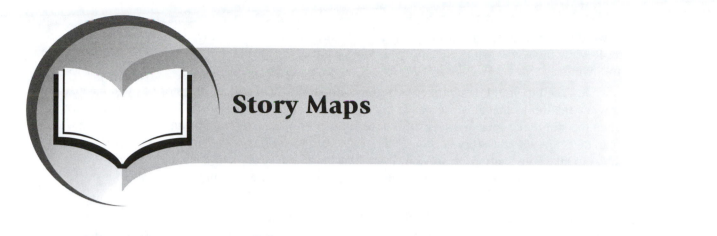

Story Maps

FOCUS		TEXT		WHEN			WHY									HOW			
Comprehension	Vocabulary	Narrative	Informational	Before Reading	During Reading	After Reading	Predicting	Connecting	Questioning	Using Text Structure	Visualizing	Inferring	Summarizing	Synthesizing	Determining Importance	Individual	Partner	Small Group	Whole Group
•		•				•				•	•				•	•		•	•

DESCRIPTION

Understanding the elements of narrative text structure is an essential part of comprehending stories. One way for students to visualize how stories are organized is through Story Mapping. Story Maps are typically graphic organizers that have a place for the elements of narrative texts: setting, characters, events, problem, and solution. There are many ways that stories can be mapped, one of which is a Story Face (Staal, 2000). The Story Face is a graphic organizer that helps students visualize, identify, understand, and remember story elements by organizing story elements like a face.

Teaching Goals

1. To help students identify the elements of narrative text to assist comprehension.
2. To help students visualize story elements by representing story elements in a graphic organizer.
3. To provide students with a way to think about how story elements relate to each other.

Procedure

1. Select a book that has clearly identified story elements. For example, the books in the Clifford series by Norman Bridwell usually have a limited number of main characters, a clear problem, and events that lead to a resolution of the problem.
2. Make an overhead transparency of one of the Story Maps on pages 216–218 and duplicate copies for students.

3. Write the words, *setting, characters, problem, events,* and *solution* on an overhead transparency or on the board. Review the words with students and remind them of the meaning of the words. You could say the following.

> Today when I read to you, I would like you to think about the main parts of the story as you listen. Let's review the things that all stories have in common. First, there is a setting. The setting is where and when the story takes place. Stories also have characters. Characters can be animals or people. The characters are who the story is about. Stories also have a problem. The problem leads the characters to take some actions to solve it. What happens are the events of the story. The event that solves the problem is called the solution. Now that we have reviewed the main elements of a story, let's read!

4. Read the story, *Clifford Gets a Job* (Bridwell, 1965) to the students.

5. After reading the story to the group, complete a Story Map together as follows. In this example the students are using the Story Face.

> "Where did the story take place?" Students may respond, "In and around Clifford's home town." Write their responses in the circle labeled *Setting.* If students wish to add descriptive words about the setting, write them on the eyelashes above the *Setting* eye. Tell students that when you go to a place, you usually use your eyes to see what the setting looks like.

> Next ask students, "Who were the main characters in the story?" As students answer "Clifford, Emily Elizabeth, and robbers," write the names of the characters in the circle labeled *Characters.* Use the eyelashes above the character's eye for additional descriptive words or the secondary characters, *farmer* and *police.* Tell students that when you go somewhere, your eyes help you see the characters.

> Ask students to identify the problem in the story. Help them to identify that Clifford's food was costing too much money, and he was going to lose his home. He needed to find a job. Write the elements of the problem in the appropriate box representing the nose on the Story Face. Tell students that sometimes our noses cause problems, for example, when we get a cold or when we bump our nose when we are playing.

> Next, ask students to identify the main events of the story. Write each event in one of the *Events* circles representing the Story Face mouth.

>> Clifford joined the circus, but he got in trouble.

>> Clifford worked on a farm, but he wrecked the barn.

>> Clifford caught some robbers.

> Tell students, "Mouths help us know how people are feeling. Often the events that have happened in people's lives affect how they look, whether they are smiling or feeling sad."

> Finally, ask students, "What was the solution to Clifford's problem?" When students offer that the police rewarded Clifford with dog food, write the solution in the appropriate circle.

6. To conclude the lesson, review the story elements one more time and remind students to think about the things all stories have in common. Remind them that knowing these elements will help them better understand stories when they are reading.

7. Use each of the Story Maps on pages 216–218 throughout the year to provide students with several methods of representing story elements.

References

Bridwell, N. (1965). *Clifford gets a job.* New York: Scholastic.

Staal, L. A. (2000). The Story Face: An adaptation of story mapping that incorporates visualization and discovery learning to enhance reading and writing. *The Reading Teacher, 54,* 26–31.

Story Face

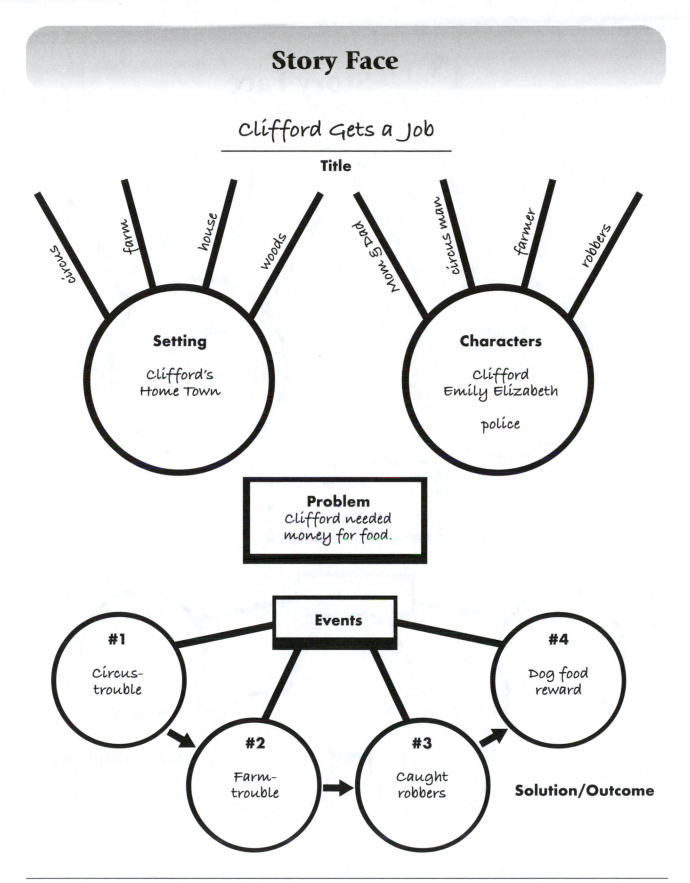

Clifford Gets a Job
Title

Setting

Clifford's Home Town

circus *farm* *house* *woods*

Characters

Clifford
Emily Elizabeth

police

Mom & Dad *circus man* *farmer* *robbers*

Problem
Clifford needed money for food.

Events

#1

Circus-trouble

#2

Farm-trouble

#3

Caught robbers

#4

Dog food reward

Solution/Outcome

Name _____ Date _____

 Story Face

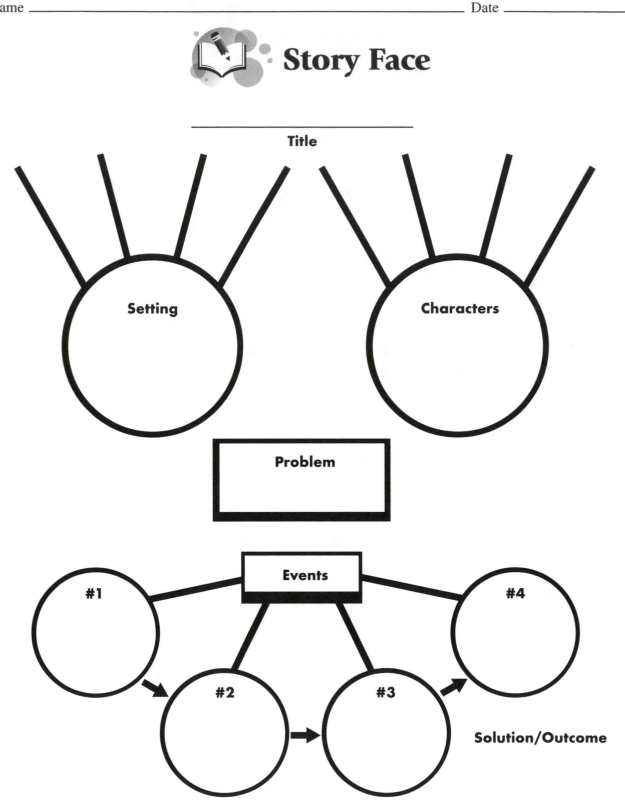

Title

Setting

Characters

Problem

Events

#1

#2

#3

#4

Solution/Outcome

Based on Staal, L.A. (2000). The Story Face: An adaptation of story mapping that incorporates visualization and discovery learning to enhance reading and writing. *The Reading Teacher, 54,* 26–31.

Jerry L. Johns, Susan Davis Lenski, and Roberta L. Berglund. *Comprehension and Vocabulary Strategies for the Elementary Grades* (2nd ed.). Copyright © 2006 by Kendall/Hunt Publishing Company (1-800-247-3458, ext. 4). May be reproduced for noncommercial educational purposes within the guidelines noted on the copyright page.

Name _____ Date _____

 **Story Map**

Title

Setting

Characters

Problem

Events

↓

↓

↓

↓

Solution/Outcome

What is this story really about?

_____

_____

_____

_____

Story Map

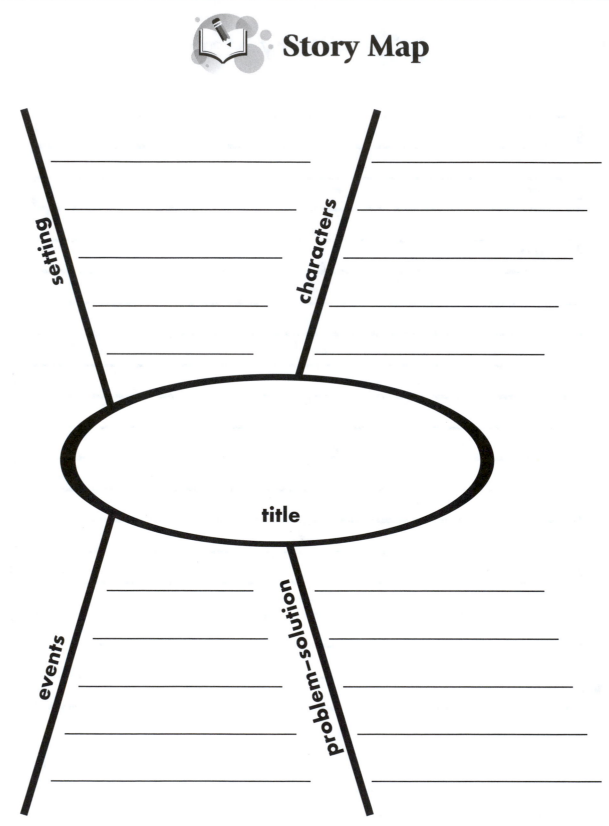

setting

characters

title

events

problem–solution

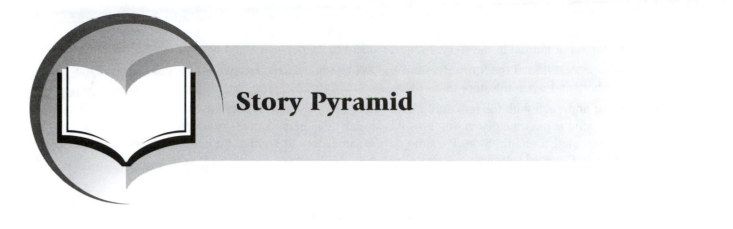

Story Pyramid

FOCUS		TEXT		WHEN			WHY									HOW			
Comprehension	Vocabulary	Narrative	Informational	Before Reading	During Reading	After Reading	Predicting	Connecting	Questioning	Using Text Structure	Visualizing	Inferring	Summarizing	Synthesizing	Determining Importance	Individual	Partner	Small Group	Whole Group
•		•				•	•						•	•		•	•	•	•

DESCRIPTION

The Story Pyramid (Waldo, 1991) is an instructional strategy to help students identify and summarize some of the major parts of a story. Like the Predict-O-Gram (see page 139), a Story Pyramid helps students learn the major features of narrative text.

Teaching Goals

1. To help students summarize stories they have read.
2. To help students make decisions about story content.
3. To encourage students to use narrative text structure to improve their comprehension.

Procedure

1. Select a story that has a clear plot outline. Read the story to students or have them read it independently.
2. Place a copy of the Story Pyramid on chart paper, the board, or an overhead transparency. Tell students that the Story Pyramid will be used to help them identify some of the major parts of the story. You might say the following.

   We have just read *Now One Foot, Now the Other* (de Paola, 1981). Notice that lines on the chart paper are in the shape of a pyramid. [Demonstrate by drawing a pyramid outside the lines with a marker.]

219

3. Draw students' attention to the word *character* under the top line. Explain that *character* refers to an important person or animal in the story. Invite a student to share a name and write it on the line.

4. Move to the second line of the Story Pyramid and ask a volunteer to give two words that describe the *setting* or where and when the story takes place.

5. Use a similar approach with the remaining lines of the Story Pyramid. After the Story Pyramid has been completed, spend some time discussing how this strategy can help students remember the story. You might also complete a second Story Pyramid for the same story to highlight other characters and events. A sample Story Pyramid follows.

Story Pyramid
Now One Foot, Now the Other by T. de Paola

<u>Bob</u>
Character

<u>home</u>   <u>years</u>
Two words that describe the setting

<u>funny</u>   <u>kind</u>   <u>teacher</u>
Three words that describe the character

<u>Bob</u>   <u>had</u>   <u>a</u>   <u>stroke.</u>
Four words to describe the problem

<u>Bobby</u>   <u>taught</u>   <u>Bob</u>   <u>to</u>   <u>walk.</u>
Five words that describe the solution

6. As students gain confidence with the Story Pyramid, divide the class into groups of three or four. Have each group identify a character in the story, the setting, and some events in the story. Then each group can share its Story Pyramid with the class.

7. Examples of blank Story Pyramids follow. Select the one that best fits your teaching situation.

References

de Paola, T. (1981). *Now one foot, now the other.* New York: G. P. Putnam's Sons.

Waldo, B. (1991). Story pyramid. In J. M. Macon, D. Bewell, & M. Vogt (Eds.), *Responses to literature: Grades K–8* (pp. 23–24). Newark, DE: International Reading Association.

 **Story Pyramid**

≋➙ **DIRECTIONS**

Fill in the blanks below to make a Story Pyramid.

_____

Character

_____ _____

Two words that describe the setting

_____ _____ _____

Three words that describe the character

_____ _____ _____ _____

Four words to describe the problem

_____ _____ _____ _____ _____

Five words that describe the solution

Name _____ Date _____

Story Pyramid

➡ DIRECTIONS
Fill in the blanks below to make a Story Pyramid.

_____
Character

_____
Two words that describe the setting

_____
Three words that describe the character

_____
Four words to describe the problem

_____
Five words that describe an event

_____
Six words that describe the solution

Jerry L. Johns, Susan Davis Lenski, and Roberta L. Berglund. *Comprehension and Vocabulary Strategies for the Elementary Grades* (2nd ed.). Copyright © 2006 by Kendall/Hunt Publishing Company (1-800-247-3458, ext. 4). May be reproduced for noncommercial educational purposes within the guidelines noted on the copyright page.

Name _____ Date _____

Story Pyramid

→ DIRECTIONS
Fill in the blanks below to make a Story Pyramid.

_____
Character

_____ _____
Two words that describe the setting

_____ _____ _____
Three words that describe the character

_____ _____ _____ _____
Four words to describe the problem

_____ _____ _____ _____ _____
Five words that describe an event

_____ _____ _____ _____ _____ _____
Six words that describe the solution

_____ _____ _____ _____ _____ _____ _____
Seven words that describe why the story was written

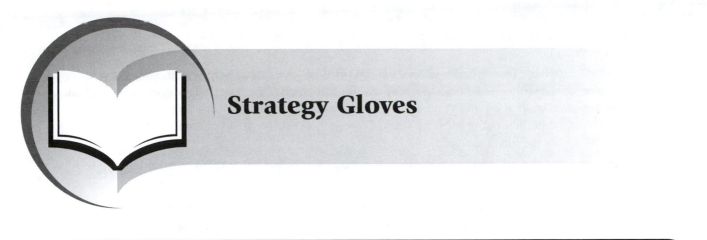

Strategy Gloves

FOCUS		TEXT		WHEN			WHY									HOW			
Comprehension	Vocabulary	Narrative	Informational	Before Reading	During Reading	After Reading	Predicting	Connecting	Questioning	Using Text Structure	Visualizing	Inferring	Summarizing	Synthesizing	Determining Importance	Individual	Partner	Small Group	Whole Group
•		•	•		•	•			•	•					•	•	•	•	•

DESCRIPTION

This multisensory approach uses visual clues, combined with teacher questioning, to place pictures on actual gloves. The questions relate to the icons and help students learn the strategy so they can use it independently during reading (Newman, 2001/2002). The goal is to help students internalize questioning strategies so they can improve their understanding of text. There are different gloves to help with narrative text (page 229), informational text (page 228), and unknown words (page 230). The informational text structure glove is explained below. It can also be used with narrative text.

Teaching Goals

1. To provide a graphic way for students to understand main ideas and supporting details.
2. To provide a graphic way for students to learn about story structure.

Procedure

1. Construct an informational strategy glove (see example on page 227). The materials needed include an inexpensive white or light colored glove, a small lock fastened in the palm of the glove, and keys fastened on each of the fingers. The lock signifies the main idea, and the keys are details that support the main idea. Newman (2001/2002) recommends using Velcro® to fasten the lock and keys on the glove. Glue the soft side of the Velcro® to the glove and attach the sticky side to the lock and keys that will be attached to the glove. Allow the glue to dry a day before attaching the items to the glove. Plastic storage bags can be used to store the glove, lock, and keys.

2. Introduce the glove to students by saying the following or adapting it to suit your mode of presentation for the book you choose.

> Take a look at what's on my hand. It's a special type of glove that can help you understand what you read. Some of the stories and books we read are informational. That means they give us facts about various topics. The lock on this glove represents the main topic and the keys represent the facts or details about the main topic or idea. As I read *Look at These Animals* (Christopher, 2003), I'm going to show you how the glove is used.

3. Show the cover of the book and invite students to predict what the book might be about. A sample class discussion follows.

> Mr. Reed: What can you tell from the cover of the book?
>
> Lacy: It's going to be about animals. I can see a dog and cat on the cover. The dog is just a puppy.
>
> Mr. Reed: Are the animals in this book real or make believe?
>
> Josh: They are probably going to be real because the pictures are of real animals.
>
> Mr. Reed: You are correct. I'll read the first couple of pages and then we will use the Strategy Glove.

4. Read the text about the animals that are called mammals. Show the pictures and have students identify the dog, cat, guinea pig, hamster, and rabbit. Then ask a volunteer to share the scientific name for the animals (mammals) and some of the characteristics they possess. A sample discussion follows.

> Mr. Reed: What is the scientific name we call these animals?
>
> Sophia: They are mammals.
>
> Mr. Reed: That's right. Look at my glove. I'm going to take the lock and attach it to the palm of the glove. The lock stands for mammals, the main idea or topic of these pages. Now look at the keys I'm holding. They stand for some of the facts or details I read about the mammals. Tell me some of those details, and I will put a key on a finger for each detail you mention.
>
> Zach: Mammals can be big or small.
>
> Mr. Reed: That's right. I will attach a key for that detail about mammals.
>
> Lacy: Mammals have hair or fur on their bodies.
>
> Cherith: And mammals make milk for their babies.
>
> Mr. Reed: Very good! I'll add a key for the fur or hair and another key for the idea that mother mammals make milk for their babies.

5. Continue reading the book. The main idea or topic of the next two pages is "birds." The details are "covered with feathers," "have wings," and "mother birds lay eggs." Invite students to offer their ideas and add the lock and keys. Clarify and reinforce as necessary.

6. As you read about fish, amphibians, and reptiles, invite students to help you identify the main idea and details for each group. You may wish to have a student wear the glove and add the lock and keys as other students share information about a particular group of animals. See page 227 for a completed Strategy Glove for amphibians.

7. Continue using the Strategy Glove with a variety of texts. Students enjoy using the actual gloves, so you may want to make several. Once students have grasped the basic idea, you could use the reproducible masters of the Strategy Gloves on pages 228–230.

8. The Strategy Glove can also be used for writing a paragraph using a main idea or topic and the details. Have students write the details for a specific topic on the fingers and then develop a paragraph from these details.

References

Christopher, G. (2003). *Look at these animals*. New York: Sadlier-Oxford.

Newman, G. (2001/2002). Comprehension strategy gloves. *The Reading Teacher, 55,* 329–332.

Strategy Glove for Informational Text

Look at These Animals by G. Christopher

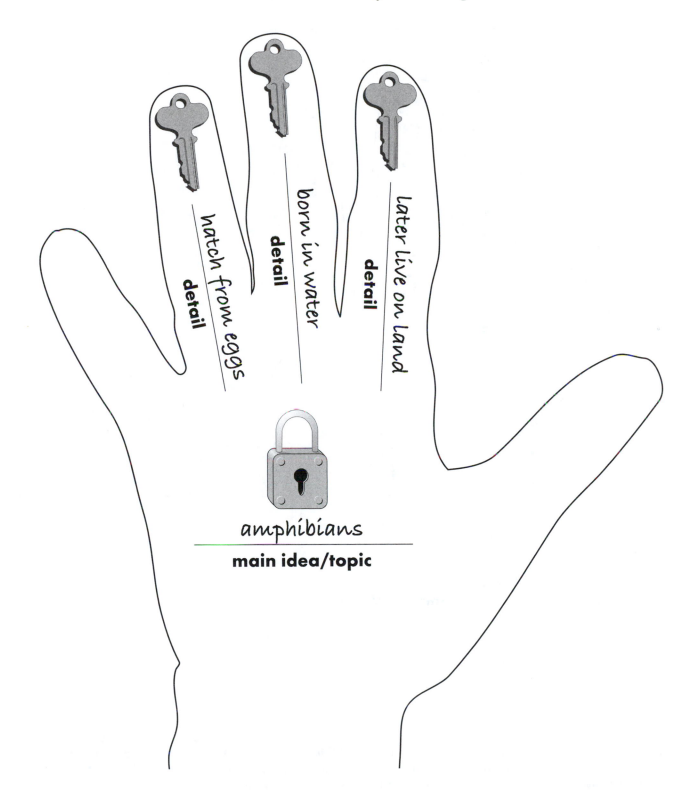

Name _____ Date _____

Strategy Glove for Informational Text

Title _____

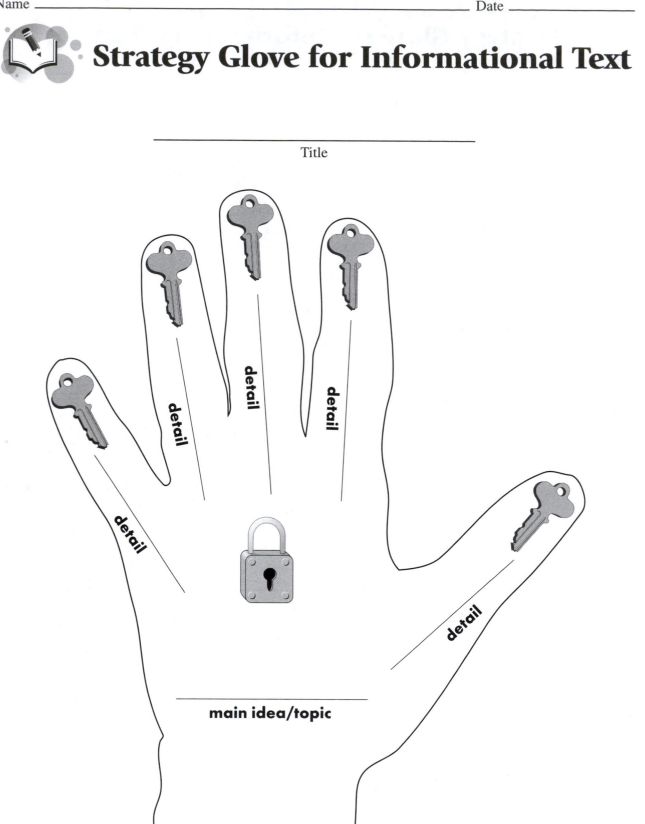

detail

detail

detail

detail

detail

main idea/topic

 # Strategy Glove for Stories

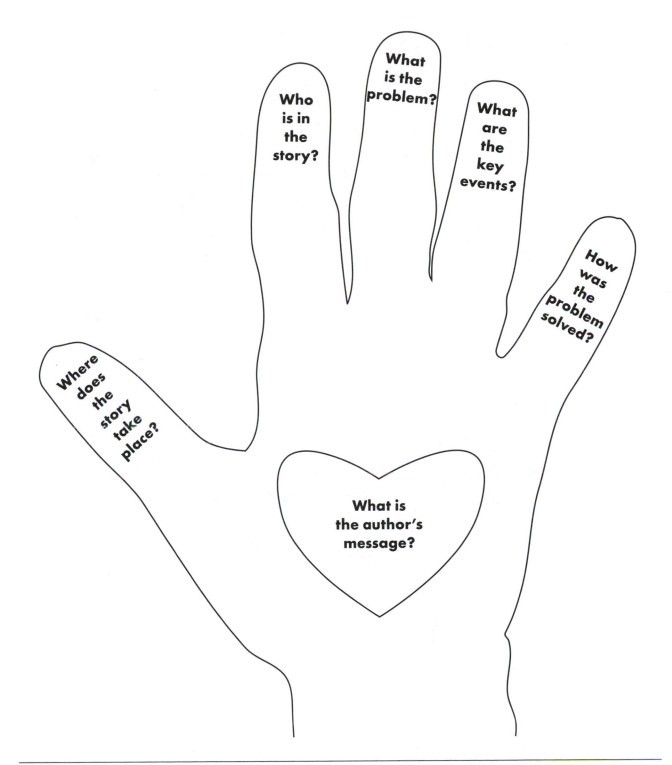

Who is in the story?

What is the problem?

What are the key events?

How was the problem solved?

Where does the story take place?

What is the author's message?

Name _____   Date _____

Strategy Glove for Unknown Words

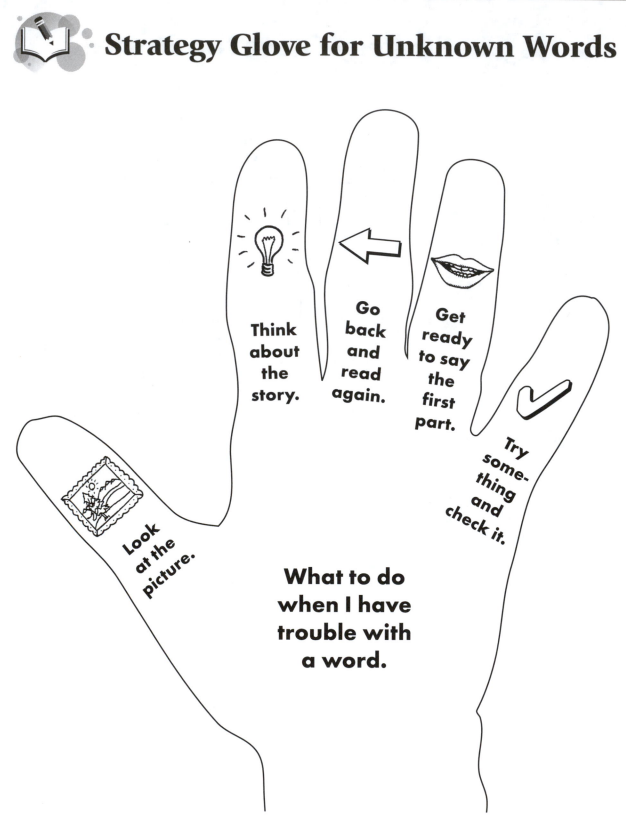

Think about the story.

Go back and read again.

Get ready to say the first part.

Try some- thing and check it.

Look at the picture.

What to do when I have trouble with a word.

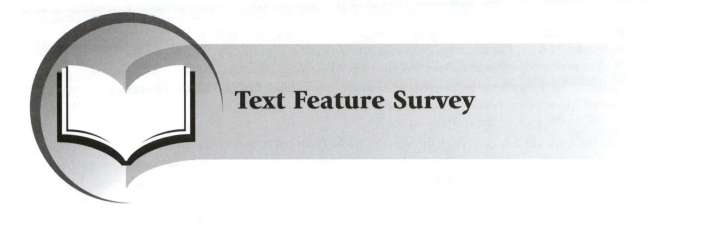

Text Feature Survey

FOCUS		TEXT		WHEN			WHY									HOW			
Comprehension	Vocabulary	Narrative	Informational	Before Reading	During Reading	After Reading	Predicting	Connecting	Questioning	Using Text Structure	Visualizing	Inferring	Summarizing	Synthesizing	Determining Importance	Individual	Partner	Small Group	Whole Group
•			•	•						•						•	•	•	•

DESCRIPTION

Informational texts have different features than do narrative texts. These text features are specialized items that authors and publishers use to help students get information from the text. Some informational texts have such features as graphs, pictures, maps, italics, titles, inserts, and tables. A Text Feature Survey can help students identify text features before reading.

Teaching Goals

1. To teach students the types of features used in informational texts.
2. To help students use text features as a comprehension aid.
3. To provide students with a tool to compare different kinds of informational texts.

Procedure

1. Explain to students that informational texts have different types of features than do narrative texts. Hold up an example of an informational text and ask students to discuss the types of features they see. Refer to the reproducible Features of Informational Text that follows on page 233 to guide students toward the types of features they might find. Write students' responses on the board. Add features to the list that students do not mention.

2. Organize the list of text features into categories such as Print Features, Graphics, Organizational Aids, and Comprehension Aids. Explain why the text feature fits into each category. You might want to make an overhead transparency of page 233 for use during the lesson.

3. Help students identify text features by using an example from a book that includes several of the features on the Information Text Features List. For example, the book *X-Zone: Mummies* (Patton, 2004) contains some, but not all, of the features on the list.

4. Hold up the book for students and page through the book. Point out the text features in the book as in the following example.

   Let's look on the first page. The book begins with the copyright page. This feature is important because it tells us when and where the book was published. We can learn that this book was published in 2004 so we can conclude that the book should contain the most recent information about the topic. Scanning through the book, we find many other text features such as a title page, an introduction, a table of contents, margin notes, pictures, captions, and so on.

5. Tell students that surveying text features is an important way to learn about a book before reading. Make a transparency of the Text Feature Survey on page 234. Show the completed example to students to illustrate how to use the survey. Then have students try the survey independently on a new book.

6. After students have successfully completed one or more Text Feature Surveys, help students identify the different features in a variety of informational texts.

7. Gather samples of different kinds of texts such as magazines, newspapers, textbooks, trade books, pamphlets, brochures, and so on.

8. Divide the class into groups of four or five students. Give each group five different kinds of texts. Ask each group to examine each text looking for different text features. Have students refer to the list of features of informational text if necessary.

9. Duplicate and distribute the Text Feature Survey on page 235. Have students write the name of the text they read in the left-hand column and its features in the right-hand column.

10. When students are finished, have them compare the groups' lists of texts and features. Remind students that different texts will have different features and that all of the features are provided to help the reader understand the information in the text.

11. Encourage students to look for text features as they read independently.

Reference

Patton, G. (2004). *X-Zone: Mummies.* New York: Scholastic.

Informational Text Features List

Print Features

Font	Bold, italics, bullets, etc.	Labels
Color	Titles	Captions
Punctuation	Headings, subheadings	Underline

Graphics

Diagrams	Sketches	Charts
Maps	Graphs	Tables
Figures	Timelines	Cartoons
Photographs	Drawings	Boxes
Sidebars	Cross-sections	Illustrations
Inserts		

Organizational Aids

Table of contents	Preface	Appendix
Index	Introduction	Glossary
Title page	Copyright information	

Comprehension Aids

Overviews	Review questions	Margin notes
Embedded questions	Purpose questions	Quizzes

Jerry L. Johns, Susan Davis Lenski, and Roberta L. Berglund. *Comprehension and Vocabulary Strategies for the Elementary Grades* (2nd ed.). Copyright © 2006 by Kendall/Hunt Publishing Company (1-800-247-3458, ext. 4). May be reproduced for noncommercial educational purposes within the guidelines noted on the copyright page.

Name _____ Date _____

Text Feature Survey

1. Write the title of the book and the name of the author.

   Mummies by Geoff Patton

2. Page through the book. What do you notice about the book's pictures, headings, subheadings, and graphics?

   This book has pictures, maps, charts, or graphs on every page. There are many margin notes and questions throughout the book.

3. Place a check (✔) by any features of the book. Write any others on the lines.

✔	Pictures with captions	✔	Graphs or charts
✔	Inserts	✔	Cartoons
✔	Table of Contents		Index
✔	Maps		Diagrams
✔	Glossary		Tables
✔	Illustrations	✔	Realistic pictures
✔	Quiz	✔	Headings, subheadings

   _____ _____   _____ _____
   (other)   (other)

   _____ _____   _____ _____
   (other)   (other)

   _____ _____   _____ _____
   (other)   (other)

4. Tell how these features help you understand this text.

   _____

   _____

   _____

   _____

   _____

   _____

Jerry L. Johns, Susan Davis Lenski, and Roberta L. Berglund. *Comprehension and Vocabulary Strategies for the Elementary Grades* (2nd ed.). Copyright © 2006 by Kendall/Hunt Publishing Company (1-800-247-3458, ext. 4). May be reproduced for noncommercial educational purposes within the guidelines noted on the copyright page.

Name _____ Date _____

 **Text Feature Survey**

1. Write the title of the book and the name of the author.

2. Page through the book. What do you notice about the book's pictures, headings, subheadings, and graphics?

3. Place a check (✓) by any features of the book. Write any others on the lines.

_____ Pictures with captions		_____ Graphs or charts
_____ Inserts		_____ Cartoons
_____ Table of Contents		_____ Index
_____ Maps		_____ Diagrams
_____ Glossary		_____ Tables
_____ Illustrations		_____ Realistic pictures
_____ Quiz		_____ Headings, subheadings

_____ _____	_____ _____
(other)	(other)
_____ _____	_____ _____
(other)	(other)
_____ _____	_____ _____
(other)	(other)

4. Tell how these features help you understand this text.

_____

_____

_____

_____

_____

_____

Jerry L. Johns, Susan Davis Lenski, and Roberta L. Berglund. *Comprehension and Vocabulary Strategies for the Elementary Grades* (2nd ed.). Copyright © 2006 by Kendall/Hunt Publishing Company (1-800-247-3458, ext. 4). May be reproduced for noncommercial educational purposes within the guidelines noted on the copyright page.

Text Talk

FOCUS		TEXT		WHEN			WHY									HOW			
Comprehension	Vocabulary	Narrative	Informational	Before Reading	During Reading	After Reading	Predicting	Connecting	Questioning	Using Text Structure	Visualizing	Inferring	Summarizing	Synthesizing	Determining Importance	Individual	Partner	Small Group	Whole Group
•	•	•				•	•	•	•		•	•						•	•

DESCRIPTION

Text Talk (Beck & McKeown, 2001; Beck, McKeown, & Kucan, 2002) is an approach to vocabulary, comprehension, and language development through the use of read-alouds. It is similar to Questioning the Author on page 165 (Beck, McKeown, Hamilton, & Kucan, 1997), but in Text Talk students listen to, rather than independently read, the text. Both procedures focus on constructing meaning. Text Talk uses the rich language of children's trade books to enhance and expand students' use of sophisticated words (i.e., those not generally in their listening or speaking vocabularies prior to the lesson).

Teaching Goals

1. To help students increase their knowledge and use of sophisticated words.
2. To encourage students to use vocabulary words in a variety of contexts.
3. To help students enlarge and enrich their listening and speaking vocabularies.
4. To encourage students to develop an interest in and awareness of words.
5. To enhance students' comprehension of text.

Procedure

Lesson Preparation

1. Select a children's trade book that contains rich language and concepts along with illustrations to help support comprehension.

2. Read the book and select 3–6 sophisticated words to teach. Sophisticated words that are useful for instruction are:
   - Typically not common in students' oral language
   - High-frequency words for mature language users
   - Typically found in written language
   - More precise labels for words students already know
   - Ones that can enhance students' language abilities
   - Often adjectives and adverbs
   - Interesting
   - Not too difficult to explain using language students will understand

3. Prepare student-friendly definitions of the selected words, telling what the words mean in everyday language.

4. Prepare examples using the words beyond the context of the story.

5. Develop activities for students to interact with and use the words in meaningful ways beyond the story by giving a variety of examples that expand students' understanding beyond the story.

6. Select stopping points in the text where students will be invited to respond, check predictions, and make new predictions about the story.

Sample Lesson

Book: *The Wednesday Surprise* (Bunting, 1989)
Synopsis: Anna stays with Grandma on Wednesday nights. Together they plan a special surprise for Dad's birthday.

Sophisticated Words to Teach: 1. Vague
                                 2. Nervous
                                 3. Astonished

Before Reading

1. Show the cover of the book and ask students to make predictions based on the title and cover illustration.

During Reading

2. Read the story aloud without showing the pictures. If some vocabulary words are critical for student understanding of major story content, explain them briefly as they are encountered in the text. For example, in this book the father goes to basketball practice at the Y. If students are unfamiliar with what Y means, stop reading and explain briefly that it is a building where people go to play sports and exercise.

3. Invite student reactions and comments about the story by asking them to turn and talk to a partner at specific stopping points in the text. Also invite students to make new predictions about what they think will happen next in the story.

4. Finish reading the story aloud.

After Reading

5. Invite student comments and reactions.

6. Have students retell the story using the pictures for support.

7. Discuss any further connections or reflections students share.

Text Talk

1. Use the sophisticated words previously selected for instruction. The first word is *vague*.

2. Contextualize the meaning by saying the following.

   In the story, Grandma *vaguely* answers Mom's questions about being there for Dad's birthday dinner. She acts as if she has almost forgotten about it.

3. Explain the meaning through a student-friendly definition by saying the following.

   Vague means that an idea isn't clear. If you answer a question *vaguely,* people may not understand what you mean. Let's say the word together aloud, *vague*.

4. Give examples beyond the story by saying the following.

   Suppose someone visiting our school asks a student for directions to the office. If the student doesn't tell the visitor clearly where it is, the visitor might not find the office because the directions were *vague*.

   When someone answers a question, but doesn't give all of the necessary information in a clear way, the answer is *vague*.

5. Provide guided meaningful interactions by offering choices. You might say the following.

   I'll say some sentences. If any of the things I say are examples of something being *vague,* you say, *vague*. If something is not an example of being *vague,* don't say anything.

   Knowing exactly what to do. (Students should remain quiet.)

   Not being sure what the homework assignment is. (Students should say *vague*.)

   Not telling everything you know about something. (Students should say *vague*.)

   Being confused about directions for building a model. (Students should say *vague*.)

6. Bring closure to the word *vague* by saying the following.

   What's the word we use when something isn't clear? Let's say it together, *vague*.

7. Focus on the second word previously selected for instruction, *nervous*.

8. Contextualize the meaning by saying the following.

   In the story, Anna is *nervous* when she is waiting for Grandma to share her birthday surprise.

9. Explain the meaning of *nervous* by saying the following.

   Nervous means you can't relax. You may feel like you can't sit still or you can't concentrate. Let's all say the word aloud together, *nervous*.

10. Give examples beyond the story by saying the following.

Sometimes, when you are worried about something, you feel *nervous*. If you don't know what is going to happen, the uncertainty can make you *nervous*. Perhaps going to the dentist might make you feel *nervous* or you might feel *nervous* if you think you might get called to the principal's office.

11. Provide guided meaningful interactions by asking questions or inviting students to provide reasons or examples. You might say the following.

What might make you feel *nervous,* soft music or loud music? Why?

When might you feel *nervous?* When you know your Mom will be on time to pick you up or if you think she may have forgotten you? Why?

What makes you *nervous?* You might say, "I feel *nervous* when . . ."

12. Bring closure to the word *nervous* by saying the following.

What's the word that means we can't relax or we feel worried? *Nervous.*

13. Go on to the third sophisticated word previously selected for instruction, *astonished.*

14. Contextualize the meaning by saying the following.

When Grandma begins to read to the family, Mom, Dad, and Sam are all *astonished.*

15. Explain the meaning of *astonished* by saying the following.

Astonished is how you feel when you experience a very great surprise.

16. Give examples beyond the story by saying the following.

I remember when my aunt came home from a trip and she brought a new husband with her! I was *astonished!*

I remember when my friends gave me a surprise birthday party. When I came home, they all jumped out and yelled, "Surprise!" I was *astonished* because I had not expected anyone to be there.

17. Provide guided meaningful interactions by asking students to act it out or give examples. You might say the following.

Make a face to show how you would look if you felt *astonished.*

Tell us about a time when you felt *astonished.*

18. Bring closure by saying the following.

What is the word that means how we feel if we have just experienced a huge surprise? Say it aloud with me, *astonished.*

19. Bring the lesson to a close by asking students to use all three words in the same context. You might say the following.

We talked about three words today that were in our story. Those words were *vague, nervous,* and *astonished.*

If you went to a restaurant with your family and the menu appeared to be *vague,* what might that be? What could you do to make it clear?

After the server explains the menu, you may not know whether the macaroni and cheese you ordered will be just like what you eat at home. How would you feel? Why?

When your food arrives, you get the biggest bowl of macaroni and cheese that you have ever seen. How would you feel?

Elements of a Text Talk Lesson: A Summary

1. Introduce the book.
2. Read the book aloud.
3. Present each sophisticated word as used in the context of the story.
4. Provide a student-friendly definition of each word.
5. Give examples of how the words are used beyond the context of the story.
6. Provide opportunities for students to participate in guided meaningful interactions with each word.
7. Bring closure by having students use all of the words.

Extending the Learning

After words have been taught through a Text Talk lesson, it is important to maintain them in the classroom. They may be incorporated into classroom life by any of the following means.

- Class Word Jar
- Word Wizard Bulletin Board
- Class Dictionary (containing words, their meanings, sample sentences, and illustrations)
- Student Writing
- Charts (showing tally marks for each time a word is used)

5-Day Plan for Using Text Talk

Day 1
Introduce a book, read it aloud, and do Text Talk lesson.
Day 2
Practice vocabulary in additional contexts.
Day 3
Introduce a new book, read it aloud, and do Text Talk lesson.
Day 4
Practice vocabulary in additional contexts.
Day 5
Review Text Talk words of the week and have students do activities with the words. These might include sentence completions, matching words and their meanings, comparing how words are alike and different, drawing words from the Class Word Jar and creating sentences with the words or assessing students' word knowledge.

References

Beck, I. L., & McKeown, M. G. (2001). Text talk: Capturing the benefits of read-aloud experiences for young children. *The Reading Teacher, 55,* 10–20.

Beck, I. L., McKeown, M. G., Hamilton, R., & Kucan, L. (1997). *Questioning the author: An approach for enhancing reading engagement with text.* Newark, DE: International Reading Association.

Beck, I. L., McKeown, M. G., & Kucan, L. (2002). *Bringing words to life: Robust vocabulary instruction.* New York: Guilford.

Bunting, Eve. (1989). *The Wednesday surprise.* New York: Clarion.

Text Talk Lesson Plan

Title: _____

Author: _____

Sophisticated Words: _____ _____

_____ _____ _____

_____ _____ _____

Word _____ **Page** _____

Student-friendly Definition:

Word in Context:

Examples in Other Contexts:

Meaningful Interactions:

- Questions
- Alike & Different
- Examples & Nonexamples
- Sentence Stems
- Choices
- Associations
- Act It Out
- Reasons

Closure—Using All of the Words
- One Context for All the Words   • Students Create Examples   • Same Format for All the Words

Maintaining the Words
- Wondrous Words Bulletin Board
- Class Word Jar
- Daily Message
- Class Dictionary
- Writing
- Tally Use
- Vocabulary Notebook

Jerry L. Johns, Susan Davis Lenski, and Roberta L. Berglund. *Comprehension and Vocabulary Strategies for the Elementary Grades* (2nd ed.). Copyright © 2006 by Kendall/Hunt Publishing Company (1-800-247-3458, ext. 4). May be reproduced for noncommercial educational purposes within the guidelines noted on the copyright page.

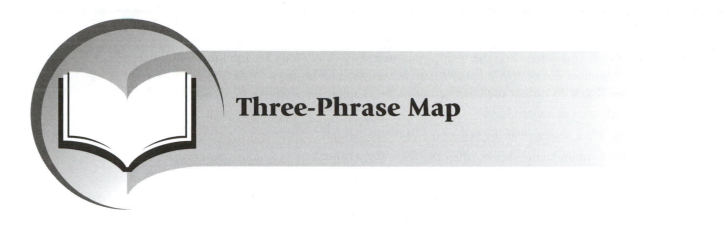

Three-Phrase Map

FOCUS		TEXT		WHEN			WHY									HOW			
Comprehension	Vocabulary	Narrative	Informational	Before Reading	During Reading	After Reading	Predicting	Connecting	Questioning	Using Text Structure	Visualizing	Inferring	Summarizing	Synthesizing	Determining Importance	Individual	Partner	Small Group	Whole Group
•			•			•							•	•	•	•	•	•	•

DESCRIPTION

A Three-Phrase Map helps students identify the main idea of an informational text selection. The main idea of a text can sometimes be found in one sentence, but more often the main point of a text needs to be generated by a reader. When students think of the concept of main idea more broadly, they are generally more successful in identifying what is important in the selection and what can be considered the main idea.

Teaching Goals

1. To help students understand that informational text selections have a main point.
2. To assist students in identifying ideas that contribute to the main idea of an informational text selection.
3. To help students synthesize ideas to form one main idea.

Procedure

1. Identify an informational text to use to demonstrate determining a main idea in the selection. There are many types of informational texts that are not written like textbooks. One example is *You Wouldn't Want to be a Medieval Knight* by Fiona Macdonald (2004). This book is written in second person and it provides information about medieval times.

2. Identify a section of the book that has an easily identifiable main idea. *You Wouldn't Want to be a Medieval Knight* is divided into sections that can be easily used to model the Three-Phrase Map.

3. Duplicate and distribute blank copies of the Three-Phrase Map that can be found on page 247.

4. Write the term "main idea" on the board. Ask students whether they are familiar with the term. Have students volunteer their knowledge of main idea. After students have expressed what they know, add to that knowledge with further explanations as in the example that follows.

Teacher: What is a main idea?

Student: It's a sentence at the beginning of the paragraph.

Teacher: Can the main idea be other places in the writing?

Student: I'm not sure.

Teacher: Actually, the main idea of a text can be stated in the first sentence but it can also be part of the entire piece. The author may not have stated it in one sentence. If the main idea is in one sentence, what will it do?

Student: The main idea will tell what the paragraph is about.

Teacher: Yes, the main idea expresses the main point of the paragraph or page.

5. Explain to students that when they read they should gather thoughts about the main idea. Tell students that for the Three-Phrase Map they will be generating three thoughts from the text that express the main point.

6. Read a selection from *You Wouldn't Want to be a Medieval Knight* to students. For example, you might read the part about "Life in the Castle." Ask students to generate ideas that they glean from the text. Write the phrases on the board. Some examples follow.

> Expensive to build
>
> Needs constant repairs
>
> Needs guards
>
> Castles are big, and they have private rooms.
>
> Castles are cold, drafty, and smelly.

7. After students have written their three words or phrases, ask them to think about the main idea of the reading. In this example, the main idea could be that castles are uncomfortable to live in. Accept other ideas that students can justify from their selected thoughts. Have students write the main idea in the box under the circles.

8. Have students identify three of the ideas to write in the circles of the Three-Phrase Map. Phrases, sentences, or words can be used to record each ideas.

9. Remind students to think about the main idea of informational text as they read independently.

Reference

Macdonald, F. (2004). *You wouldn't want to be a medieval knight*. Danbury, CT: Scholastic Library.

Name _____ Date _____

Three-Phrase Map

Author _____ Title _____

Phrase #1

Phrase #2

Phrase #3

Main Idea

_____

Name _____ Date _____

Three-Phrase Map

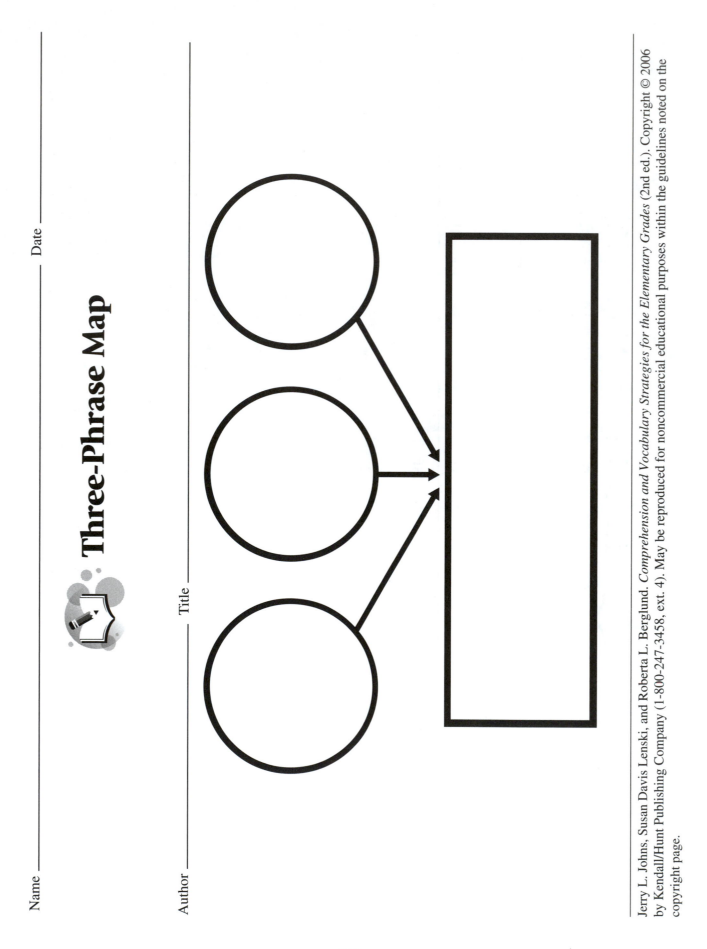

Title _____

Author _____

Tiered Bingo

FOCUS		TEXT		WHEN			WHY									HOW			
Comprehension	Vocabulary	Narrative	Informational	Before Reading	During Reading	After Reading	Predicting	Connecting	Questioning	Using Text Structure	Visualizing	Inferring	Summarizing	Synthesizing	Determining Importance	Individual	Partner	Small Group	Whole Group
•	•	•	•	•	•	•	•	•	•	•		•	•	•	•	•			

DESCRIPTION

Students need opportunities to make choices about the reading and writing strategies that they use. Choice about activities provides students with an understanding that they can learn to become independent strategic readers. A strategy that promotes reading choices is Tiered Bingo (Tomlinson, 1999). Tiered Bingo has another benefit: you can differentiate the strategies that you ask students to use.

Teaching Goals

1. To help students internalize the reading strategies they have learned.
2. To encourage students to make choices about the strategies they use.
3. To help students develop a sense of choice during reading.

Procedure

1. Identify several reading and writing strategies and activities that you would like students to accomplish over a number of days. Prepare a range of activities from those that would challenge your best readers to those that could be completed independently by readers who struggle.
2. Duplicate the reproducible master of Tiered Bingo on page 254 and write the activities you have selected on the blanks. Vary the activities by level of difficulty.

3. Tell students that they will be using Tiered Bingo during independent work time for several days. Explain to students that they will be allowed to choose activities to accomplish. Say something like the following.

> Today we're going to do something different in our classroom. You're going to get the chance to decide which activity you want to complete each day. If you are making your own decision, the student sitting next to you might be working on a different activity than you are, so don't let that surprise you.

> It will be something like when you're getting ready to play soccer. Before the game, some of you practice kicking the ball, some of you practice shooting, and some of you practice passing the ball to a friend. Your team is doing several different things at once. That's what will happen when our class does Tiered Bingo.

4. Review with students how to play Bingo. You might use a Bingo sheet with numbers or letters so that students can practice playing. Decide whether you want to award prizes or points for students who make a Bingo or whether you want students to complete a certain number of squares. If you have developed activities with a range of difficulties, however, you should not ask students to complete the entire Tiered Bingo sheet.

5. Explain what each of the activities in the squares means. You might use icons or pictures for some activities so students can use the strategies independently.

6. Sample Tiered Bingo sheets using reading and writing activities, one with reading strategies, and a reproducible master of Tiered Bingo follows on pages 251–254.

Reference

Tomlinson, C. A. (1999). *The differentiated classroom: Responding to the needs of all learners.* Alexandria, VA: Association for Supervision and Curriculum Development.

Tiered Bingo

Read an ABC book.	Write a letter to a friend.	Read the room.
Use magnetic letters to make 10 new words.	Read a book from your basket.	Listen to a story on tape.
Write the first and last names of 6 students.	Write the capital and lower case letters of the alphabet.	Write a story about your family.

Tiered Bingo

Write a prediction you made while reading.	Write connections using Brain Surfing.	Find some new vocabulary words as you read. List them here.
After reading, sketch how the book make you feel.	Draw a picture of the main character.	Make a Story Map.
Question the Author while reading. Write your question here.	Create a Story Pyramid.	Fill out Four Square on a new word.

Tiered Bingo

Tiered Bingo

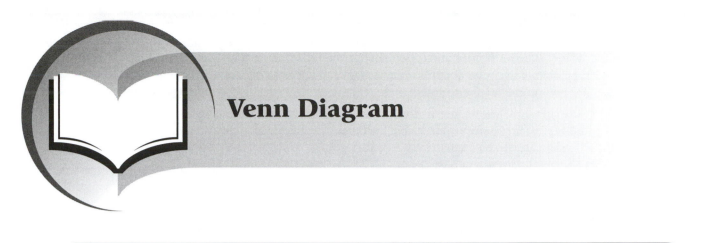

Venn Diagram

FOCUS		TEXT		WHEN			WHY									HOW			
Comprehension	Vocabulary	Narrative	Informational	Before Reading	During Reading	After Reading	Predicting	Connecting	Questioning	Using Text Structure	Visualizing	Inferring	Summarizing	Synthesizing	Determining Importance	Individual	Partner	Small Group	Whole Group
•		•	•	•	•	•	•						•			•	•	•	•

DESCRIPTION

The Venn Diagram helps students to organize information in a visual way. Through the use of a Venn Diagram, students can compare and contrast two or more ideas, themes, characters, or issues being studied. When the Venn is completed, students may create a written summary of the major points. By using a Venn Diagram, students can organize and evaluate information and then use the completed diagram as a vehicle for writing. Venn Diagrams can also be used before reading to make predictions about text.

Teaching Goals

1. To help students organize information.
2. To help students make comparisons and contrasts among two or more topics.
3. To help students summarize information.

Procedure

1. Select one or more books, book chapters, major concepts, or a film and a book that you wish students to read and/or view.

2. When students have finished reading, listening to, or viewing the information, choose a topic and invite students to consider the similarities and differences in the information presented about that topic. For example, students may have read about hurricanes and tornadoes in the book, *Extreme Weather* (Phelan, 2004). You might say the following.

> We have just read about severe storms that occur in our country as well as in other parts of the world. In the United States, these storms are called hurricanes and tornadoes. Let's consider some of the ways these storms are alike and also how they differ.

3. Distribute copies of a two-topic Venn Diagram (see page 258) or draw a Venn Diagram to be viewed by the entire group.

4. Write *Hurricanes* on the line above one of the circles and *Tornadoes* on the line above the other circle.

5. Explain to students that they should think about what they know about both of these extreme storms that was confirmed from their reading or viewing. If an idea is true for both hurricanes and tornadoes, they should write the idea in the center where the two circles overlap. Ideas that relate to either storm, but not both, should be written under the appropriate headings. For example you might say the following.

> In our reading today, we learned that storms need warm, moist air to develop. Let's list this idea in the center of our diagram where we put the ideas that are the same for both hurricanes and tornadoes. However, we also learned that tornadoes produce the fastest winds on Earth, faster than those in a hurricane. We should list this fact in the circle under Tornadoes.

6. Invite students to work to complete their Venn Diagrams, using the information from their text. You may wish to do one or two more examples with the group until you are confident that they understand how to proceed on their own in subsequent lessons.

7. When students have completed their diagrams, ask them to look at the information they have recorded on their diagrams and summarize verbally or in writing how hurricanes are like tornadoes. Then ask them to explain how they differ.

8. Additional Venn Diagram reproducibles can be found on pages 258–263.

Reference

Phelan, G. (2004). *Extreme weather.* Washington, DC: National Geographic Society.

Name _____

Date _____

✏ Venn Diagram

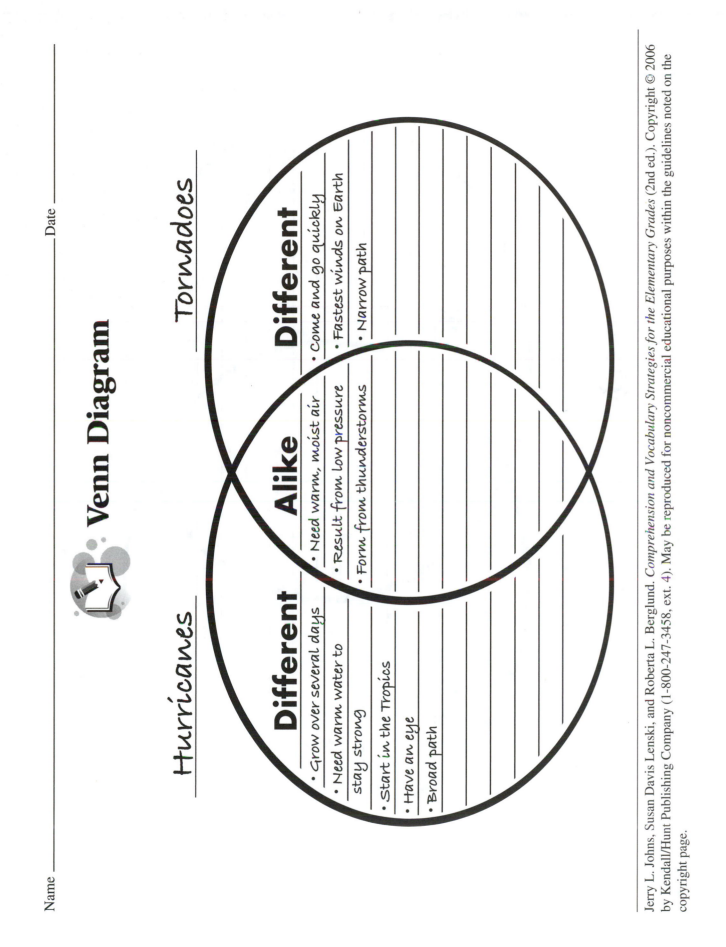

Hurricanes _____

Tornadoes _____

Different
- Grow over several days
- Need warm water to stay strong
- Start in the Tropics
- Have an eye
- Broad path

Alike
- Need warm, moist air
- Result from low pressure
- Form from thunderstorms

Different
- Come and go quickly
- Fastest winds on Earth
- Narrow path

Name _____

Date _____

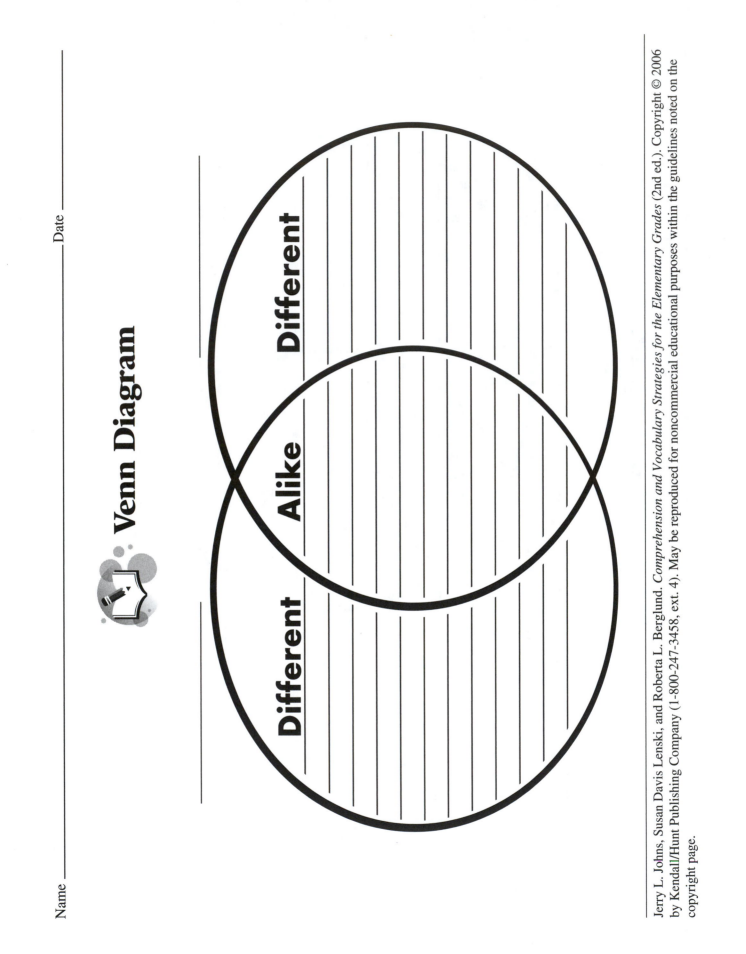

Venn Diagram

Different

Alike

Different

Name _____ Date _____

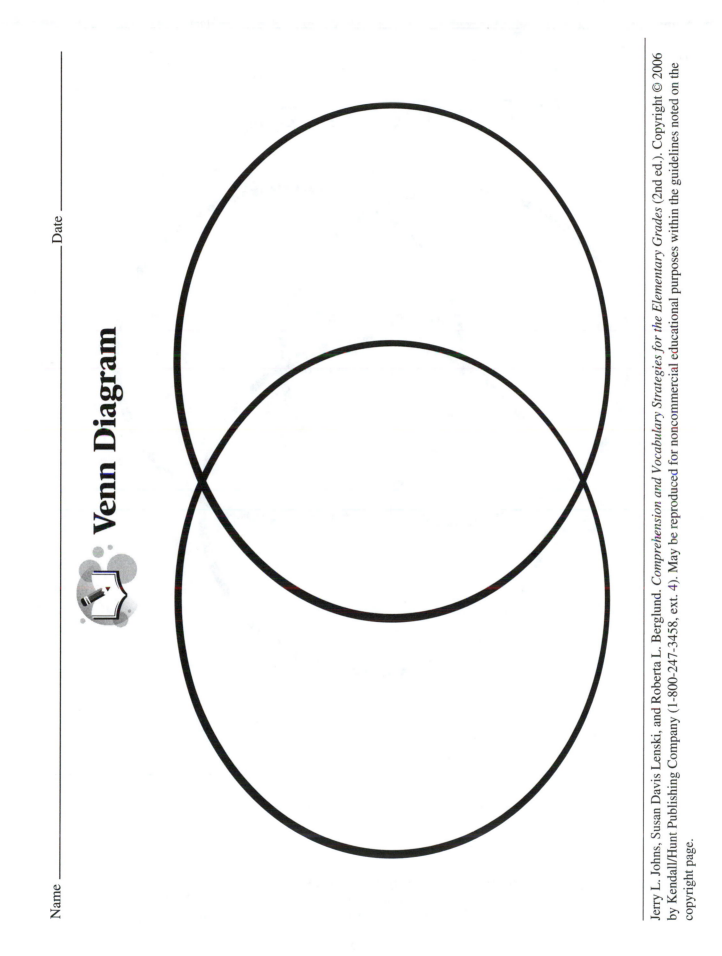

Venn Diagram

Name _____ Date _____

Topic/Concept: _____

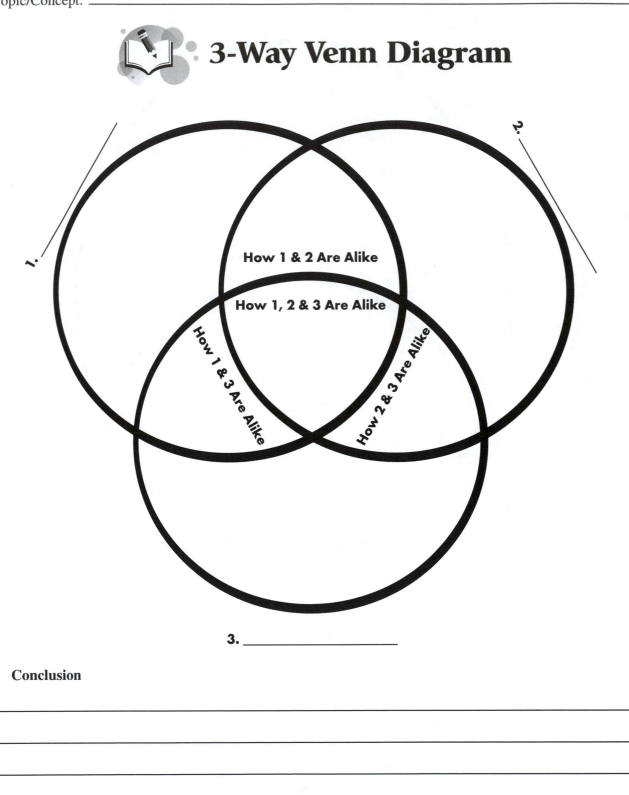

3-Way Venn Diagram

1.

2.

How 1 & 2 Are Alike

How 1, 2 & 3 Are Alike

How 1 & 3 Are Alike

How 2 & 3 Are Alike

3. _____

Conclusion

_____

_____

_____

_____

Name _____ Date _____

Topic/Concept: _____

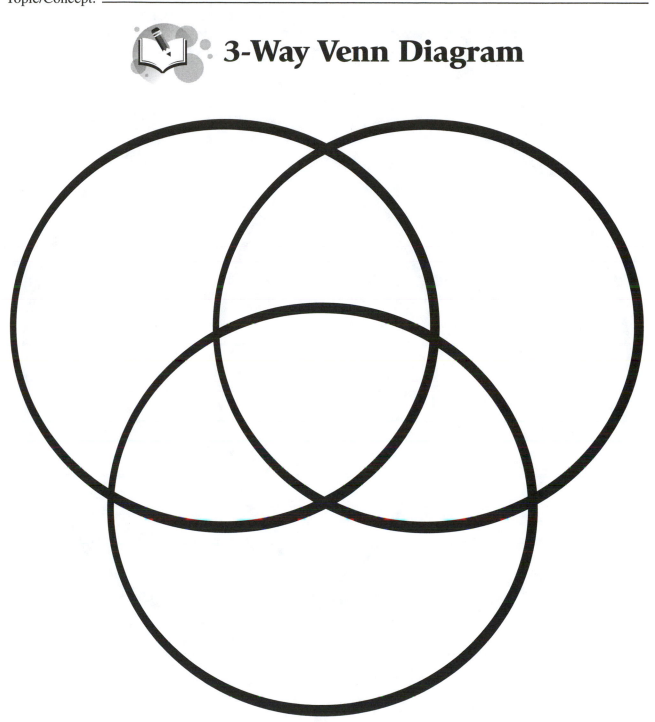

3-Way Venn Diagram

Name _____ Date _____

Topic/Concept: _____

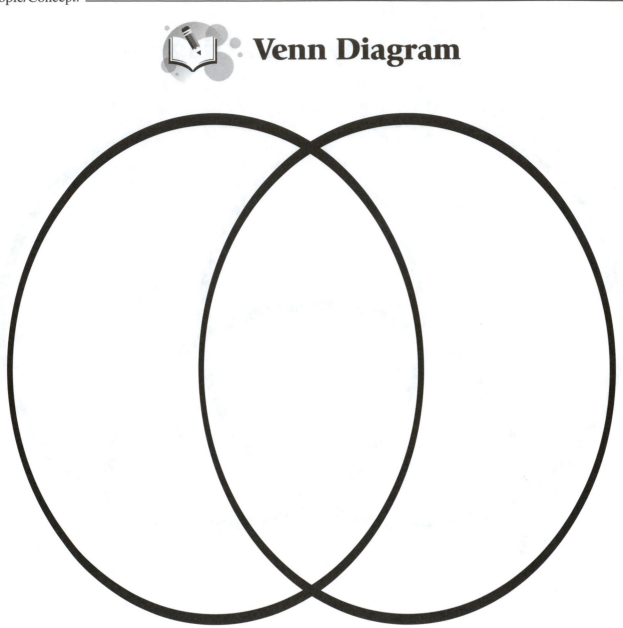

Venn Diagram

Conclusions/Connections/Questions/Realizations . . .

Name _____ Date _____

Venn Diagram

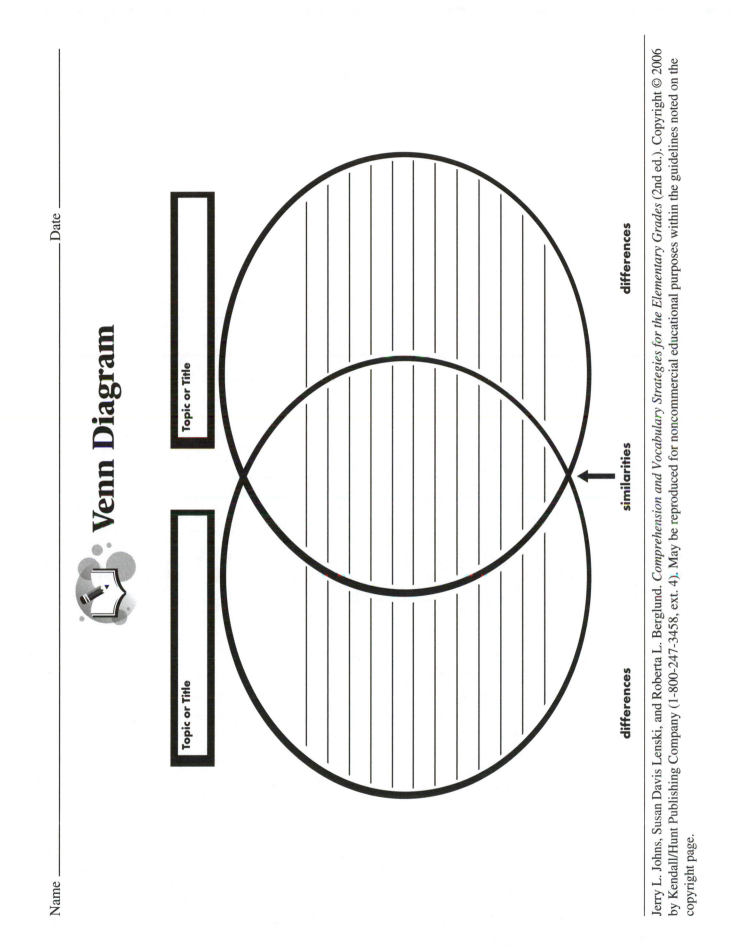

Topic or Title

Topic or Title

differences

similarities

differences

Vocabulary Anchors

FOCUS		TEXT		WHEN			WHY									HOW			
Comprehension	Vocabulary	Narrative	Informational	Before Reading	During Reading	After Reading	Predicting	Connecting	Questioning	Using Text Structure	Visualizing	Inferring	Summarizing	Synthesizing	Determining Importance	Individual	Partner	Small Group	Whole Group
	•		•	•			•	•										•	•

DESCRIPTION

Vocabulary Anchors (Winters, 2001) provide a visual organizer to assist students in actively exploring, connecting with, and using content vocabulary. Vocabulary Anchors are best used to introduce new terms that are not highly complex or abstract and for which students may have strong prior conceptual knowledge and association. Vocabulary Anchors provide a student-friendly means of helping students access and use their background knowledge to build connections from the known to the new.

Teaching Goals

1. To help students make connections between known and new words.
2. To guide students in identifying similar and distinguishing characteristics of words.
3. To help students understand and remember new vocabulary.

Procedure

1. Display a drawing or picture of a boat that appears to be floating on water. You may want to introduce the concept of Vocabulary Anchors using the example below.

   Most of you have seen boats floating on lakes or rivers near where we live or perhaps when you were on vacation. Many of you may have experienced being in a boat when it was floating. When boats are near the dock, they are usually tied to a post or raised out of the water to keep them from floating away. Sometimes when we are out in boats, far away from the dock, we want to stay in one place for awhile and there is nothing near us to tie the boat to. Does anyone know how you keep a boat in one spot and keep it from drifting when you are floating out in a river or lake? [Elicit from students that an anchor is one means of keeping a boat from drifting.] Does anyone know how the anchor is connected to the boat? [Elicit from the students that the anchor is attached to the boat with a chain, rope, or strong line called a tethering line.]

2. Explain that when we are learning something new, it helps to have something to connect our new ideas to. Connecting helps to keep them from drifting away, just like an anchor holds a boat in one place and keeps it from drifting away.

3. Present the boat and anchor graphic organizer (see page 269) and say the following.

    An anchor connected to the boat helps it stay in one place and keeps it from drifting away. We can use our experience with anchors to help us develop a way to remember new words or ideas in our reading and keep them from drifting away from us. We are going to call this drawing a Vocabulary Anchor. We can use Vocabulary Anchors to help us connect things we already know with things we are learning. This will help us remember them.

4. Present an example on an overhead transparency and model your thinking process for students as you complete the graphic organizer. For example, draw a boat or make a transparency of the graphic organizer on page 269 and write the term *orangutan* within the bottom of the boat. Then write a word that is similar to *orangutan* that students are likely to know inside the anchor beneath the boat, for example, *chimpanzee.* Tell students that this is an anchor word that helps you know something about the new boat word. Connect the two with a line to show that the anchor is connected to the boat. You might say the following.

    We are going to be learning about a kind of ape called an *orangutan.* We are going to call our new word our boat word. Here is a word I already know that might be something like our boat word. It's *chimpanzee.* I'm going to call that word our anchor word. *Orangutans* and *chimpanzees* are similar in that they both are *apes.* They are also *warm-blooded* and they can use their *thumbs* to grasp things, just like we do. I am going to write the words that help me know that *orangutans* and *chimpanzees* are similar right next to the tethering line connecting our anchor to our boat. I am going to put a plus (+) next to those words.

5. Write the words *apes, warm-blooded,* and *thumbs* adjacent to the tethering line and place a plus (+) before each word (see example on page 268).

6. Now describe how the two terms are different. As you describe these critical differences, write the words away from the boat and anchor, allowing them to float away from them. Put a minus (–) next to these words. You might say the following.

    Our boat word and our anchor word are not exactly alike. Let me tell you some ways that they are different. Orangutans live in Asia, while chimpanzees live in Africa. Also, orangutans are slow-moving and they live alone, while chimpanzees can move quickly and prefer to live in large groups of fifty or more. Because these words help us know how the terms *orangutan* and *chimpanzee* are different, I am going to write them like they are floating out away from our boat and anchor. I am going to put a minus (–) next to these words.

7. Write the words *Asia, slow-moving,* and *alone* in the space near the right side of the boat. Put a minus (–) in front of these words.

8. Turn your attention to the sail on the boat and ask the following question.

    What words might we write on the sail of our boat to help us remember our new boat word, *orangutan?* Words that we choose may be different for each of us, based on the experiences we have had. We all use our experiences to help us remember new words and ideas.

9. Ask one or more students to suggest words to put on the sail, explaining how these words will help them remember the new word. To model, you might share some words that you would use and explain why you chose them, perhaps sharing a memorable experience that helps you connect with the word. You might also draw a picture instead of, or in addition to, one or more of the words added to the sail.

> I remember going to the zoo with my nieces and we saw an orangutan. In fact, we saw a mother orangutan with a baby. She was holding it very close to her and swinging on a vine through the trees. Because of my memory, I am going to write *baby* and *vine* on my sail to help me remember the mother orangutan that I saw. Perhaps one of you could help me add pictures to my words by drawing a baby ape and a vine. When I look at my Vocabulary Anchor, I have lots of ways of remembering about *orangutans*. When I read more about apes, I might be able to add some more ideas to my boat picture.

10. Finally, review the Vocabulary Anchor with students and explain how students can use it to help them learn and remember a new term.

> Let's look at our boat again. The new word we want to learn and remember is written on our boat. It's our *boat word*. The anchor is a word that we already know that is something like our new word. It helps us connect what we already know to our new word. The words near the tethering line help us know how these two words are alike. The words floating out in the water away from the boat help us know how our *boat word* and our *anchor word* are different. Each of us can add words or pictures to the sail, based on things we already know, to help us remember our new *boat word* in our own special way.

11. As students become more familiar with the use of Vocabulary Anchors, you might provide them with partially-completed Vocabulary Anchors for some of the key vocabulary words in a specific chapter or unit. Students may also enjoy selecting words that should be *boat words* for a specific unit of study. This strategy can also be linked to Vocabulary Self-Collection on page 277.

Reference

Winters, R. (2001). Vocabulary anchors: Building conceptual connections with young readers. *The Reading Teacher, 54,* 659–662.

Vocabulary Anchors

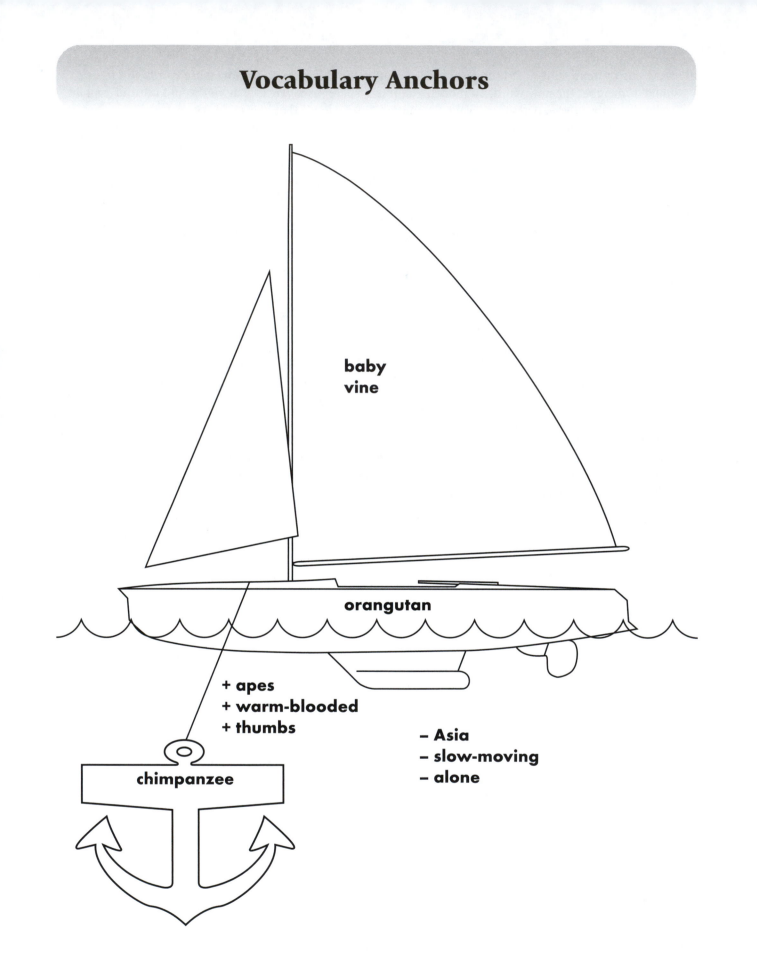

baby
vine

orangutan

+ apes
+ warm-blooded
+ thumbs

– Asia
– slow-moving
– alone

chimpanzee

Name _____ Date _____

Vocabulary Anchors

Based on Winters, R. (2001). Vocabulary anchors: Building conceptual connections with young readers. *The Reading Teacher, 54,* 659–662.

Name _____ Date _____

 Vocabulary Anchors

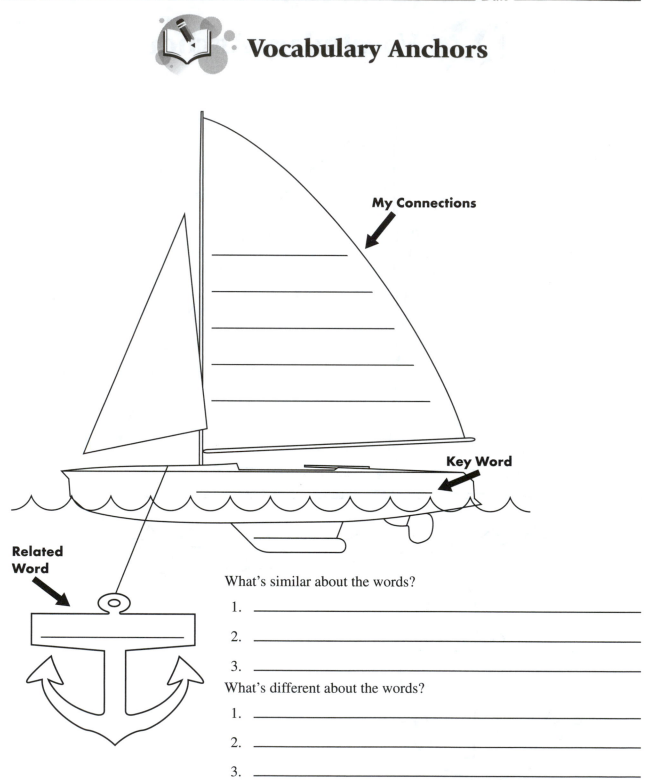

My Connections

Key Word

Related Word

What's similar about the words?

1. _____

2. _____

3. _____

What's different about the words?

1. _____

2. _____

3. _____

Based on Winters, R. (2001). Vocabulary anchors: Building conceptual connections with young readers. *The Reading Teacher, 54,* 659–662.

Jerry L. Johns, Susan Davis Lenski, and Roberta L. Berglund. *Comprehension and Vocabulary Strategies for the Elementary Grades* (2nd ed.). Copyright © 2006 by Kendall/Hunt Publishing Company (1-800-247-3458, ext. 4). May be reproduced for noncommercial educational purposes within the guidelines noted on the copyright page.

Vocabulary Four Square

FOCUS		TEXT		WHEN			WHY									HOW			
Comprehension	Vocabulary	Narrative	Informational	Before Reading	During Reading	After Reading	Predicting	Connecting	Questioning	Using Text Structure	Visualizing	Inferring	Summarizing	Synthesizing	Determining Importance	Individual	Partner	Small Group	Whole Group
•	•	•				•		•		•						•	•	•	•

DESCRIPTION

Vocabulary Four Square, as described in Johns and Berglund (2006) and Lenski, Wham, Johns, and Caskey (2006), is a vocabulary strategy to help students learn meanings for words. One key element of the strategy is having students make a personal association or connection with the word. Such a connection may enhance vocabulary acquisition and aid in the retrieval of the word's meaning when it is encountered in print.

Teaching Goals

1. To help students learn new word meanings and enlarge their vocabularies.
2. To encourage students to make personal connections to new vocabulary words.
3. To help students develop personal responsibility for vocabulary learning.
4. To encourage students to create visual images of vocabulary words.

Procedure

1. Draw a square with four quadrants on the board or chart paper. Label each of the quadrants as shown in the example below. For older students, you can make an overhead transparency of the appropriate Vocabulary Four Square reproducible master.

Word	My Connection
What It Means	**Picture or How It Looks**

2. Model the strategy using a vocabulary word selected from a text students will read or use the example from *Weather Tools* (Lowell, 2003) that follows. You might model the strategy by saying the following.

   Today we will be reading a book to help us learn about the weather. I've selected a word from the book. [Print *thermometer* in the upper-left quadrant and invite a student to pronounce the word.] Notice that there are three other squares on the chart. [Point out the squares.] When we complete the four squares, you will know more about the word.

3. Then have students share their ideas about the word's meanings. Following the reading of the book, write a brief definition of *thermometer* in the lower-left quadrant of the Vocabulary Four Square and read the definition to the group.

4. Have a student read the phrase in the lower-right quadrant. Then have students share descriptions of *thermometer* that could be used to draw a picture or an illustration. When the sharing is completed, make a sketch of a *thermometer* in the lower-right quadrant. A student could also be asked to draw the illustration.

5. For the upper-right quadrant, tell students something like the following.

   To help you remember *thermometer,* make a personal connection or clue to help you remember the word. Each of you may have a different connection. My connection is that we have an indoor/outdoor thermometer in our home. What personal connection can you make with *thermometer* or what helps you think of *thermometer?* [Have students share their connections in small groups or with a partner. Then ask for volunteers to share with the class. Stress that connections, by their very nature, are unique and personal.]

Word	My Connection
thermometer	We have an indoor/outdoor thermometer at home.
What It Means	**Picture or How It Looks**
It tells how hot or cold it is.	

6. Use Vocabulary Four Square several more times with the whole class to help students gain a working knowledge of the strategy. When students gain confidence with the strategy, share copies of the reproducible master on page 274 with students and guide them in completing the sheet individually or in small groups. Words chosen should be important in understanding the lesson you are teaching. The terms *rain gauge* and *wind sock,* for example, might be possible words for a unit on weather tools.

7. One variation of Vocabulary Four Square is to substitute *Opposite* for *Picture or How It Looks* in the bottom-right quadrant. The reproducible master on page 275 contains this option, so you can choose the reproducible master that is most appropriate for your use.

References

Johns, J. L., & Berglund, R. L. (2006). *Strategies for content area learning* (2nd ed.). Dubuque, IA: Kendall/Hunt.

Lenski, S. D., Wham, M. A., Johns, J. L., & Caskey, M. (2006). *Reading and learning strategies: Middle grades through high school* (3rd ed.). Dubuque, IA: Kendall/Hunt.

Lowell, M. (2003). *Weather tools.* New York: Sadlier-Oxford.

Vocabulary Four Square

Word	My Connection
What It Means	**Picture or How It Looks**

Vocabulary Four Square

Word	Personal Clue or Connection
Definition	**Opposite**

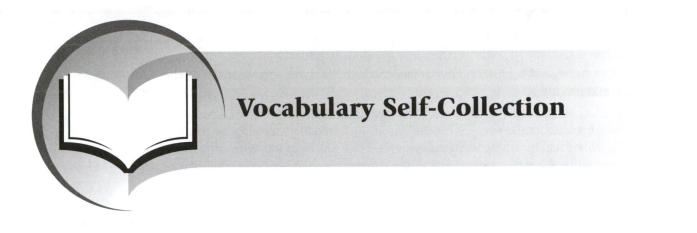

Vocabulary Self-Collection

FOCUS		TEXT		WHEN			WHY									HOW			
Comprehension	Vocabulary	Narrative	Informational	Before Reading	During Reading	After Reading	Predicting	Connecting	Questioning	Using Text Structure	Visualizing	Inferring	Summarizing	Synthesizing	Determining Importance	Individual	Partner	Small Group	Whole Group
•	•	•				•		•							•	•	•	•	•

DESCRIPTION

Students learn new vocabulary terms through instruction, but they should also be encouraged to discover new words while they are reading independently. One strategy that helps students become aware of new words while reading is the Vocabulary Self-Collection Strategy (VSS) (Haggard, 1986). Vocabulary Self-Collection heightens students' awareness of unfamiliar words and provides them with practice in learning new words in their natural contexts.

Teaching Goals

1. To provide a systematic means for students to enlarge their vocabularies.
2. To help students develop word consciousness.
3. To provide an opportunity for students to determine important words to learn.
4. To help students develop personal responsibility for vocabulary learning.

Procedure

1. Tell students that they learn new words in many ways and that independent reading is one of the ways students can learn new words. Emphasize that knowing the meanings of many words will help students become better readers. Also explain that becoming aware of new words can enrich students' vocabularies.

2. Explain to students that there is a strategy that can help them become aware of words as they read: Vocabulary Self-Collection. Write the name of the strategy on the board.

3. To begin this strategy, demonstrate how to independently look for new words in reading. An example that you could use follows.

> I was reading the book *Emily* (Bedard, 1992) last night because I wanted to read it to our class. It's a children's book about the poet Emily Dickinson. As I read the book, I came to a word that I didn't know: *parlor.* I had heard the word many times, but I wasn't exactly sure what it meant. I decided that the word *parlor* was a word that I wanted to learn. I also thought it would be a good one for our entire class to learn.

4. After you have modeled finding a new word, provide students with a story to read that has some unfamiliar words. Have students read the book and write down words that intrigued them. For example, if students read the story *Emily,* they might choose the following words: *plucked, wilted, hedge, bulged,* and *rascal.*

5. Divide the class into groups of three or four students. Have students share their lists of individually selected words with their group and instruct the group to choose one word to present to the rest of the class.

6. Have each group share the word that they selected. Write the words on the board or on an overhead transparency. Conduct a vote for one word from the list for the class to learn.

7. Duplicate and distribute the Vocabulary Self-Collection reproducible master on page 279. After students have selected a word from the class list, have them find the word in its context in the story and write it on the sheet. Then have students predict a definition from the context in which the word occurs. Finally, have them check on the accuracy of their definition with a dictionary or glossary. An example follows.

Word	Sentence Where I Found the Word
Parlor	"Glasses chimed through the open parlor door below."
Predicted Definition	**Definition**
A living room	A room used for visitors.

8. Encourage students to record new vocabulary words found during reading using the Vocabulary Self-Collection reproducible master on page 280.

References

Bedard, M. (1992). *Emily.* New York: Scholastic.

Haggard, M. R. (1982). The vocabulary self-collection strategy: An active approach to word learning. *Journal of Reading, 26,* 203–207.

Haggard, M. R. (1986). The vocabulary self-collection strategy: Using student interest and word knowledge to enhance vocabulary growth. *Journal of Reading, 29,* 634–642.

Name _____ Date _____

Vocabulary Self-Collection

Title _____ Pages _____

Word _____	Sentence Where I Found the Word _____
Predicted Definition _____	Definition _____

Word _____	Sentence Where I Found the Word _____
Predicted Definition _____	Definition _____

Word _____	Sentence Where I Found the Word _____
Predicted Definition _____	Definition _____

Vocabulary Self-Collection

WORD	SENTENCE FROM THE TEXT/DEFINITION

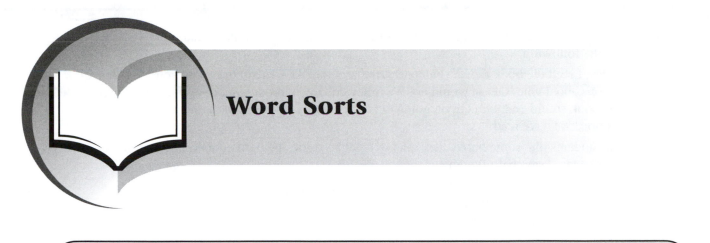

Word Sorts

FOCUS		TEXT		WHEN			WHY									HOW			
Comprehension	Vocabulary	Narrative	Informational	Before Reading	During Reading	After Reading	Predicting	Connecting	Questioning	Using Text Structure	Visualizing	Inferring	Summarizing	Synthesizing	Determining Importance	Individual	Partner	Small Group	Whole Group
•	•	•	•	•	•	•	•		•	•						•	•	•	•

DESCRIPTION

Sorting words (Gillet & Kita, 1979) is a classification strategy that helps students organize and remember vocabulary and concepts. Before, during, and/or after reading, key words are clustered into categories that are either determined by the teacher or developed by the students. Another way Word Sorts can be used is to help students identify text patterns in informational texts. Most informational texts are organized by a combination of five patterns: main idea/detail, sequence, cause/effect, problem/solution, and comparison/contrast. Opportunities for comprehension are increased if students can follow the logic of the text by understanding the way the thoughts are organized. A lesson demonstrating this use follows.

Teaching Goals

1. To help students understand some of the ways ideas or words in informational text can be organized.
2. To engage students in identifying main ideas and details.
3. To help students explore different informational text structures.

Procedure

1. Remind students that stories are organized by a story grammar: plot, setting, characters, and theme. Review the terms if necessary.

2. Tell students that readers use their knowledge of text organization when they read. For example, you might say the following.

> Yesterday, I read the book *Olivia* (Falconer, 2000) to you. As we read the book, you made lots of predictions about what Olivia would do. We followed Olivia through her day, and you even predicted that the book would end with Olivia going to bed. The story followed the same pattern as lots of other stories we have read.

3. Explain to students that some books they read will not be stories but will contain information. For example, you could say the following.

> We also read another kind of story yesterday, a book about pigs on the farm. That book was not a made up story. It gave us information about pigs. Remember how we compared the book *Olivia* to the book about pigs?

4. Guide students to understand how narrative stories differ from informational text. An example of a classroom discussion follows.

> Mr. Starkey: How were the books *Olivia* and the book about pigs different?
>
> Jane: *Olivia* was a made-up story and the pig book wasn't.
>
> Mr. Starkey: How else were they different?
>
> Adam: *Olivia* didn't have any facts to learn.
>
> Mr. Starkey: Any other differences?
>
> Sheila: The pictures in the pig book were real.

5. Select an informational book to use to teach students text organization. Some books that seem to be informational books, such as *A Picture Book of Christopher Columbus* (Adler, 1991), are really narratives because they tell a story. Look for books that are not a story but that *explain* things.

6. Once you have selected an informational book, identify the text's organizational pattern. Most books written for young children will be written in the main idea/detail pattern.

7. Identify the main idea of a page or paragraph from the text. For example, you could use the section on Columbus's ships from the *Atlas of Exploration* for this activity. The main idea from that section is "Columbus took three ships on his journey west."

8. Make the Word Sort cards. On one of the cards, write the key words from the main idea sentence: Three ships. Then identify details from the paragraph and write them one per card. Examples could include Nina, Pinta, Santa Maria, tall-sided, three masts, large sails, and Columbus. A sample set of Word Sort cards can be found on page 283.

9. Read the selection to students or have students read independently. Tell students to look for the ways the text is organized.

10. Duplicate the word cards, cut them apart, and distribute them to students. Instruct students to arrange the cards in the order of the paragraph. Students should begin with the card "Three ships." Reinforce the idea that the first card is the main idea of the entire paragraph.

11. Provide students with many demonstrations and examples, emphasizing that informational texts are organized differently from fictional texts and use Word Sorts to illustrate how texts are organized.

12. Word Sort reproducible masters can be found on pages 284–285.

References

Adler, D. (1991). *A picture book of Christopher Columbus.* New York: Scholastic.

Falconer, I. (2000). *Olivia.* New York: Atheneum.

Gillet, J., & Kita, M.J. (1979). Words, kids and categories. *The Reading Teacher, 32,* 538–542.

Starkey, D. (1993). *Atlas of exploration.* New York: Scholastic.

Word Sort Cards

Atlas of Exploration by D. Starkey

Three ships	Nina
Tall sides	Large sails
Three masts	Pinta
Columbus	Santa Maria

Word Sort Cards

—————————————————————————

Title and Author

Name _____ Date _____

 **Word Sort Cards**

_____
Title and Author
